They've walked a mile for a camel, played the outhouse blues in Outer Mongolia, and hobnobbed with the Seyfu of Wuli. They've traveled by elephant, kayak, luxury yacht and "flying ghetto" to earth's remotest corners. And now Oswald and Mary Pillsbury Lord tell the incomparable—uncensored—and totally absorbing story of their adventures throughout Africa, Asia and a world that nobody knows: *Exit Backward, Bowing.*

Gambia . . . Sikkim . . . Nepal . . . Muscat . . . from sultans to salamanders, they've seen it all: VIP "connections"—thanks to Mrs. Lord's distinguished career in the United Nations—and native living —courtesy of insatiable curiosity and old-fashioned "guts." It's the greatest trip since Marco Polo visited Cathay, and it's told with rare perception and unfailing humor: from a near-disastrous audience with Emperor Haile Selassie to "roughing it" in the muttonous monotony of Outer Mongolia; from a luxurious cruise 250 miles into the heart of darkest Africa to an inch-by-inch tour of the Persian Gulf on a steamer crammed with 1,320 sweating Hindus and Moslems and 2 Lords (also sweating). They were present, fifth row center, at the coronation of the King and Queen of Sikkim; they were also present —originally front row center, a position they soon lost—when the visit of Britain's Queen Mother to Kenya inspired a seating crisis among the local British dowagers. "If only the Yale line could charge like Englishwomen at the sight of royalty!"

But travel to the Lords means becoming acquainted with each country in a way

(Continued on back flap)

Exit Backward, ~ Bowing ~

by Oswald B. Lord

WITH THE ADVICE AND DISSENT OF

Mary Pillsbury Lord

DRAWINGS BY ROY DOTY

THE MACMILLAN COMPANY
COLLIER-MACMILLAN LTD., LONDON

THE MACMILLAN COMPANY
866 Third Avenue, New York, N.Y. 10022
Collier-Macmillan Canada Ltd., Toronto, Ontario

Library of Congress Catalog Card Number: 74-122291
First Printing
Printed in the United States of America

Contents

6 *Contents*

Introduction

MARY and I were bumping in our Land-Rover across the tundra of Outer Mongolia at the end of an interesting and long day. There were no camels or other life to be seen. The landscape had become familiar. We began to reminisce about our experiences.

We recalled moments of hushed beauty and heartwarming friendliness. We talked of all the laughs we had had and the occasional moments of danger. It had all been so much fun that we decided then we would like to share it with you.

By actual count we have traveled in one hundred and eight countries but we have included in this book only some of those in Asia and Africa. We have confined ourselves to little-known countries like Gambia, Sikkim, Nepal, Muscat, and Outer Mongolia—or to out-of-the-ordinary experiences in better-known countries like Ethiopia and the Congo.

We have had audiences with Emperor Haile Selassie and the Seyfu of Wuli. We have cruised 250 miles into the heart of Africa on a luxurious yacht and down the Persian Gulf on a steamer with 1,320 Hindus and Moslems on the decks.

Our personal contacts have been as international as our travels. During her eight years as U.S. Representative on the United Nations Commission on Human Rights, Mary made friends in many countries. Their number was enlarged through her service as a delegate or alternate delegate to the UN General Assembly during these same years.

As a result, on many of our trips we have been fortunate in seeing the world neither as tourists nor as VIPs but something in between. Though we have frequently been guests of heads of state or ambassadors, we have seldom been official guests. This happy circumstance has put us in a unique position. Not only have we learned a great deal of confidential information, but many of our experiences have been unusual. Very little of what is included here will be found in other "Travel Books."

Though I have actually written the book, Mary has shared in it completely. Not only have I quoted from her letters and drawn information from them, but her fantastic memory has been invaluable.

She would have liked me to include more names of the hundreds of people of all races, nations and colors who have been so good to us over the years. I felt that names do not interest the average reader. Her dissents have been wise and I have deleted a number of paragraphs. For instance I left out the sentence where I said I thought Nehru was a sanctimonious hypocrite.

This is in no sense a diary nor does this book have a theme or a message. Our only purpose is to entertain you.

OSWALD B. LORD

Part One

~

1

Exit Backward, Bowing

THOUGH we could see that the lion on the doorstep was chained, it was also apparent that we would have to pass well inside the radius of the chain to cross the threshold of Emperor Haile Selassie's palace in February 1959.

We had been carefully coached on the procedures we were to follow upon presentation to his Majesty by Mr. Baldanza of our Embassy, whom we had known before in Afghanistan. We had rehearsed in our room at the Ghion Hotel, lining up abreast with Mary in the middle, our son, Charlie, on her left and I on her right. We practiced all three bowing together from the waist as we entered the room, again halfway down the room, and a third time in front of our son Winston's picture on a chair at the end of the room. We had also practiced bowing three times while walking *backward* out of the room.

I have always thought Mary an unusually slow walker but there was nothing sluggish about the way she got inside the palace.

After a short wait in a small, beautifully furnished anteroom, the Emperor's secretary, who had welcomed us upon arrival, reappeared to take us to his Majesty. As we walked down the long hall we saw him standing at the far end of a large room. There was, of course, no mistaking him. He stood erect and dignified in his army uniform with rows of medals on his left breast. Though short, he was an impressive figure. His ascetic face with its coal-black hair and bristling beard had become familiar to the people of the world when he defied Mussolini and fought to prevent Italy's shameful rape of his country.

As we entered the reception room we all three bowed deeply from the waist with my giving the cue. We repeated our bows halfway down the room and again before his Highness. We had been told that it was most unusual for him to ask his visitors to be seated but he immediately motioned us toward three easy chairs drawn up at his right.

When we were all seated, the conversation was carried on in French. The Emperor understands English but prefers not to be at a disadvantage with his guests. He seemed pleased to learn that Charlie was in the Air Force and asked politely what I did. I told him I was vice-president of Galey and Lord, a textile firm. His main conversation was with Mary, as he was and is very much interested in the health and welfare of his people. As a former president of the National Health Council she was able to give him a great deal of information.

We had been told that our interview would probably last only about five minutes and that when it was to be terminated, the Emperor would raise his hand to his eyebrow as a signal to his secretary, who would see us out. Half a dozen times Haile Selassie raised his hand—but only to stroke his mustache. At each false alarm I started to rise to my feet, only to sit down again. When he finally touched his eyebrow, I was caught napping.

As we lined up in front of him preparatory to the first of our three exit bows, his secretary held out a red velvet cushion on which lay three open boxes, each bearing a solid gold medal about the size of a fifty-cent piece. A likeness of the Emperor was stamped on each one.

He made a little speech and presented each of us with this souvenir of our audience with him. We bowed and then started walking backward out of the room. Halfway we bowed again. As we did so I heard a dull thump on the soft rug. I had not closed my box properly and my medal had fallen out!

Mary and Charlie had heard the noise and realized what happened. I could tell by their facial expressions. But I wasn't going to abandon my newly received medal. My bow became more of a genuflection as I groped with my left hand until I found it.

After this unrehearsed pause we continued our retreat, still facing the Emperor. Unfortunately, my embarrassment had thrown me a little off course. Only Mary and Charlie backed through the door. My progress was checked by the door jamb. I thought I detected a slight smile on the Emperor's lips.

Addis Ababa is a very hilly city at an altitude of over seven thousand feet. One of the Emperor's palaces is at an elevation one thousand feet higher than the other. He is apt to use this cooler palace in summer.

One side of one of the main streets is devoted to the manufacture of beds and bedding. The other side of this street is the red-light district. It is known locally as "Mattress Lane" because the mattresses are made on one side of the street and used on the other.

We took two trips out into the country, one to Bis-

choustu, overlooking a beautiful lake, and another on the
Ambo Road. Most of the country houses are made of mud
with thatched roofs which leak heavily in the rainy season.
Many of them are decorated with inverted bottles to dress
them up.

One night after dinner with the Baldanzas we went to
see some marvelous native dancing in a new night club
the government had built to impress the delegates to a
meeting of the Economic Commission of Africa.

The performance was by a troupe recently organized to
perpetuate the native Ethiopian dances. Unlike most folk
dances these were not repetitious or boring but well diversified because of their different tribal influences. There
were warrior dances with men in lion skins brandishing
spears—love dances with men and women—and best of all
the women alone. They were as graceful as they were
beautiful and seemed to be bubbling over with suppressed
laughter. The Ethiopian girls use their necks much as Thai
and Balinese dancers use their hands.

We flew out of Addis Ababa via Ethiopian Airways on
the most colorful plane I have ever seen. It had a big lion
painted on the nose and the sides were streaked with
orange and yellow. We could see the Ghion Hotel. The
following year Mary was to be lying on the floor in that
hotel with gunfire below and through her bedroom window and shells passing overhead. She was in Addis Ababa
as a delegate to a United Nations seminar.

While Emperor Haile Selassie was in South America
in December 1960, the palace guard seized control of the
government and put the little known Crown Prince in
power. Mary wrote at that time:

"Up early. Telephones not working—queer. Arrived at
meeting in theater. Mme. Lefaucheux of France whispered to me *'C'est une révolution.'* Our Ethiopian chairman, Mme. Senedu, leaves the meeting 'Due to circum-

stances.' Does the calm mean the coup has succeeded or failed?

"We all go to Golf Club for luncheon as guests of Ethiopian women. At the airport we notice that planes are spaced all over the field so that the Emperor's plane could not land if he should try to come back. After our meeting we were returned to our hotels instead of attending a scheduled reception. We were told this was for our safety. Over the radio, we heard the Crown Prince's proclamation and the BBC broadcast from Nairobi: 'Coup d'état in Addis Ababa—no news as to who is behind it—all ministers in jail.'

"At 2 A.M. that morning, Wednesday, December 14, 1960, the revolutionaries had called in two generals, the chief of staff and the head of the ground forces, and told them of the coup. They pretended to go along but returned to the First Division and exhorted the men to remain loyal to the Emperor. *They* did, but the real question was, 'What would the Air Force do?'

"Thursday, 2:35 P.M. Shooting has started. Decided to go to the lobby—crossed the glass-enclosed corridor—bullets in garden—revolutionary troops creeping through bushes around the hotel, shooting at Emperor's loyal First Division on hill—we are in direct line of fire between opposing forces—may have to take to cellar.

"4:00 P.M. Shooting, terribly close. Went up to room to get more film and some bourbon. Joined two others on second-floor balcony facing field where revolutionary troops are moving mortars. Watched shooting until bullets came too close for comfort. Got downstairs in time to see a big explosion in garden. Army store near Ras Hotel up in smoke. Another hit—windows shaking. All roads are blocked. We are completely encircled. Here come the jets flying low over First Division. Some say Air Force is for the revolution and is giving warning to the First Division to surrender, others, that they are reassuring the First. If they bomb, we go to cellar, where there are blankets, candles and provisions. Plane drops leaflets, I rush out and get one.

"The pamphlet says, 'Stay with Emperor. Bodyguard give up by tomorrow noon, or we will bomb you. False propaganda is being given you. Emperor will arrive tonight. Stay with him.'

"Water is off—electricity off—boy brought me a candle—explosions all around us—we hugged the walls—everyone calm—a little girl started to sing Christmas carols—I came up to my room in lull. Now terrible shooting—hitting all sides—excuse my writing—there goes a big one! Am flat on floor trying to keep away from windows.

"Quiet. Shooting has stopped. Back on my bed writing. Darn it! Have to lie flat—piece of cement near my window just fell in from a bullet. Most of my writing is not too cohesive—but no one will ever know the noise and strain. Tracer bullets are going by the window. I get up my nerve every now and then to peek. Most are spending the night in the cellar but I do not relish finding my way there in the dark. Am now on the floor outside my bathroom door, writing this, sipping bourbon and wrapping some small presents to give to some of my friends tomorrow. I have promised one to the little eight-year-old New Zealand girl. She is very brave but I wish she would stop singing Christmas carols.

"My cubbyhole is safe unless the big guns start or until the jets (loyal or not?) start bombing. God! A real big one—the whole building shook. . . . I think we have been hit. Senator Georgette Ciselet of Belgium has just joined me. She isn't afraid of the bullets but boys started to attack her as she lay in the hall. That last blast was her window across the hall—smashed in. Now there is a lull again and I have given her one of my pillows—it's sort of crowded, as we are trying to keep our feet out of line of fire.

"When it gets light Friday morning we decide to move to cellar as firing is getting heavy. Our most dangerous run is along the glass gallery to the main building. The floor is covered with glass. There are lots of bodies in the garden and one in the pool.

"First Division tanks have left barracks on hill and are on way to the palace—the revolutionaries surrounding the hotel are shooting at them and they are returning the fire. *Here we go* . . . cross fire through the lobby. One bullet went through 'ladies' room. . . . Do I dare go? Now's the time as the one in basement is impossible. I chance it before going to the cellar. We hear planes overhead. 'Dropping leaflets,' says a Mr. Church. Boom! That's no leaflet.

"How calm and disciplined the staff is . . . no panic— cooking surrounded by windows. They served a delicious lunch in the cellar—a thick soup—fillet of beef—vegetables —and ice cream in the shape of a sitting duck. The Swiss chef has a sense of humor.

"Upstairs for a while to watch the loyal soldiers driving the revolutionaries out of the garden. They have painted white crosses on their helmets to distinguish them from the revolutionaries, who wear the same uniform. We are ordered out of the hotel while the fighting is still going on. The loyalists want to search the Ghion to see if any rebels are hiding here."

The loyalists had things pretty well under control by the next day, Saturday. Mary had lunch at the Parkers (USIS) and for the first time learned of the massacre of the cabinet ministers early in the revolt. Our ambassador, Arthur L. Richards, had gone to the palace to try to arrange a cease-fire. As he was leaving he opened the wrong door and saw twenty cabinet ministers sitting in a row—carefully guarded. He was one of the last to see nineteen of them alive. They were machine-gunned shortly afterward and only one survived. Though badly wounded, he feigned death under a pile of bodies. Killed about the same time was the man who had escorted Mary and Charlie and me to see Haile Selassie.

Mary had trouble getting back to her hotel after luncheon because the people had heard that the Emperor was returning and crowds had poured into the streets. Though the revolt had been broken, fighting continued for several days.

"Midnight Wednesday night. I thought I was through the 'exciting part' of my diary but I have everything ready again on the floor as I write this in bed. We were having dinner this evening and though we could hear shooting in the distance we thought nothing of it. Suddenly a volley of bullets came through the dining room. We all fell to the floor and crawled to the cellar. The same little girl came up to me and said with the shooting going on, 'Mrs. Lord, they are really naughty, aren't they?'

"Thursday, December 22, en route to airport. Package delivered to me this morning. What a beautiful gold bracelet. With it was a message from the Princess, the Emperor's oldest sister. Her husband, the Minister of the Interior, was the man who survived the massacre at the palace by pretending to be dead.

"An anecdote I forgot. During the heavy shooting our waiter calmly said: 'This is an international hotel—no bullets allowed here!' "

2

Musical Chairs for the Queen

THE TRIP from the airport to the city on one's first visit to a country is always an exciting experience. In Kenya, it is doubly so. Motoring into Nairobi after our flight from Ethiopia, Mary, Charlie, and I passed scores of zebras, gazelles, hartebeests, and wildebeests (the gnus of the crossword puzzles).

In addition to our trip to Kenya, in February 1959 with Charlie, we made one in January 1964 with the Julius Fleischmanns and the Ralph Haneses. As with most visitors, we were primarily interested in seeing the wild animals.

We would like to make two suggestions to anyone contemplating a trip to Kenya. Do not go to the animal park in Nairobi before you visit the large national parks where the animals really roam wild. The Nairobi park is well done and definitely superior to any zoo, but it has an air of artificiality. The animals outnumber the tourists—but not by much. The successful photographer is not one who gets a good shot of a lion but the one who snaps a lion without a car or Land-Rover in the picture.

The other suggestion is to go to the Treetops if you can get in and go there first before visiting any of the large parks. Treetops too is touristy, but a night spent there is too unique an experience to be missed.

The site of Treetops was discovered by a farmer in the 1930s. He stumbled upon a small pool and salt lick with a huge fig tree nearby. While looking around, he was charged by an enormous wild boar—which he shot. Up until then, the giant forest hogs had been mostly legendary, having been seen by few Europeans.

Word of the water hole got back to the owner of the Outspan Hotel in Nyeri, a two-hour drive from Nairobi. He conceived the brilliant idea of constructing a shelter in the giant fig tree from which hotel guests could observe the animals at sunrise and sunset and on moonlit nights.

Princess Elizabeth climbed up to Treetops a princess and came down a queen. Her father, King George VI, died that night. She became queen of England in a treetop!

We made our first trip to Treetops exactly seven years later—to the night.

But it was not the original Treetops. That was destroyed by the Mau Maus in 1954 and the giant fig tree chopped down. Since there was no other tree huge enough for the purpose, the new Treetops was built in 1957 in a cluster of several large trees. It is in a better location than the original one since it is to the west instead of the east of the water hole. As a result, the sun is not in your eyes at sunset when most of the animals appear. This is a particular boon to camera addicts.

At lunch at the Outspan Hotel, we read the rules and

instructions for Treetops. You motor a few miles by jeep but walk the last quarter mile. Every twenty or thirty yards along the path, ladders of branches are nailed to trees. If you see a wild buffalo, you are told to climb up eight feet. If an elephant is met, you must climb eighteen feet.

Only six people walk in at a time and they are covered by a gun-carrying hunter. We thought the arrangements a little theatrical at the time. But when we returned five years later, we learned that just before our second visit a wild buffalo had charged from a thicket. The hunter shot and killed him but not before he had been badly gored.

When the two parties of six had climbed the stairs into the tree house the ladder was raised for the night.

Our stealthy and nervous approach had distracted us from properly observing Treetops. It turned out to be bigger than we expected. The lower floor had a number of cubicles with beds. The walls were of bamboo and branches ran from one cubicle to another, over or under the narrow beds or out the window. There were several other "bedrooms" on the second floor, the "dining room," and the bar. The third and top floor was an observation deck.

It was a tree house beyond the dreams of the most imaginative child. And not even he or she would have conjured up the view from the windows or the top deck. There below us was the water hole. It was about a hundred yards in diameter with a clump of weeds in the center. For thirty or forty yards from the water the ground looked as though it had been newly plowed—churned up by the hooves of hundreds of wild animals. Beyond this muddy morass was a ring of hard-packed earth. Two hundred yards away was the forest. Out of the forest, leading down to the water hole, were scores of crisscrossing paths worn by animals.

You must be in Treetops before four o'clock in the afternoon so as not to frighten the animals coming to the water hole for their evening drink. At that time of day there are usually no animals to be seen except baboons. There were thirty or forty frolicking below us, including two babies who we were told were only two days old.

When baboons are not rough-housing, they are quarreling. Often mothers would turn their young bottom-side up and spank them like humans. The children love to play "pig-a-back," but usually instead of riding on their parents they hang underneath their stomachs with their legs and arms over their mothers' backs.

The baboons were not disturbed by their kinfolk. When tea was served on the observation deck some climbed trees and snatched cookies out of our hands.

Nevertheless, we were cautioned to speak in whispers or preferably not at all. As evening approached, we understood why. Animals came from the forest one by one. A bush buck, rhino, water buck, or wart hog would advance perhaps ten yards down one of the well-worn trails. Then he or she (presumably he) would look around, sniff, and perhaps retreat into the forest to reappear five minutes later, followed by his mate and often several young. It usually took about fifteen minutes for most animals to cover the two hundred yards from forest to water. They were oblivious of our presence, but concerned with watching the other animals converging on the water hole.

Seldom was there trouble between different species of animals, but two pairs of the same species would be as interested and suspicious as couples at a suburban Saturday night country club dance.

Just before sunset, as though at a given signal, all the baboons stopped their playfulness and solemnly paraded one by one down the same path into the forest with their young on their backs or clinging upside down to their stomachs. We were told they all lived in the same "village."

We descended to the self-service honor-system bar. You make your own drinks and sign your own chits.

Dinner was served on a long narrow table with a track down the middle. A delicious steak and kidney pie was put on a "flat car" on the "railroad" and pushed from one guest to another. There was no room for a waiter in our lofty perch.

If you do not see one of the big three, rhino, elephant, or wild buffalo, at Treetops, you pay nothing. We saw seven rhino but no elephants or buffalo on our first visit. It was a great experience, but our second visit was much more exciting.

Treetops was just as we remembered it. Though it had been enlarged to accommodate twenty people, we had difficulty in getting reservations for the six of us—Fleischmanns, Haneses, and Lords.

We were up in the tree before three-thirty and there were already animals there besides the ever-present baboons. None of them was drinking. A large water buck with graceful horns lay in the grass just behind our tree. To our right were three bush bucks; a family of seven wart hogs paraded by in single file with their tails held straight up like little lances. The biggest, the father, went first, then Mother, then the five children in descending order, with the smallest bringing up the rear.

In the weeds in the middle of the water hole, a beautiful large crowned crane was sitting on her eggs, occasionally turning them. Soon the male flew in to join her, his black and white wings five feet from tip to tip. He sat on the eggs for a while to relieve his mate.

Suddenly even the whispering stopped as a large rhino appeared out of the forest on the other side of the water. It was very early in the day to see one. He kept trying to find a place where it was safe for him to get a drink. Rhinos are so heavy they sometimes get stuck in the mud. He slowly circled the water hole and two hours later was directly below us.

Meanwhile more bush bucks, water bucks, and wart hogs emerged from under the trees. We were so intent on these animals and the rhino, we were all surprised when someone looked straight down and discovered two large elephants that apparently had come right under our tree house.

Soon a giant forest hog with tremendous evil-looking tusks had joined our ever-growing menagerie. Animals were coming too fast to count. Rhinos are solitary animals that travel alone and are seldom seen together except occasionally when they meet at water holes. Soon there were four of them and they started their inevitable fighting. They are "all bark and no bite" as a rule. They stand ugly face to ugly face and snort loudly but seldom attack each other. When not snorting their only other sound is like the whine of a baby.

I was the first to spot a Cape or wild buffalo coming out of the forest, followed by four more. They looked as dangerous as they are. In fifteen minutes we counted thirty-seven of them within a hundred yards of us. It began to look like the stockyards! Except by now there were eight rhinos, two elephants, four giant hogs, several dozen bush bucks, water bucks, wart hogs, etc., all unconcernedly grubbing in the mud, drinking the brown water, or watching the other animals like tourists at the Café de la Paix. All the baboons had left at sunset down the same path they had followed five years before.

The large floodlights were turned on slowly so as not to alarm the animals below us. They had first been installed for Princess Elizabeth's visit.

After cocktails and dinner we settled ourselves in large comfortable chairs on the lower veranda to enjoy the "floor show." There were no beauties but neither was there any cover charge. We were surprised that the number of animals had doubled. It looked like Times Square on New Year's Eve.

Some giant forest hogs appeared with several babies.. They charged a half dozen bush bucks and drove them away from the water. Finally the bush bucks gathered reinforcements and with two newly arrived water bucks countercharged and drove the giant hogs back into the forest.

Wild buffalo were coming from every direction. Our hunter told us there were one hundred and two there that night. Two more elephants appeared to our left and just below us, a rhino was stuck in the mud for more than an hour.

A smaller and presumably female rhino was causing a lot of trouble. The males would occasionally go beyond the snorting stage and charge each other. When they did, all the other animals would freeze motionless, except one rabbit who hopped unconcernedly about. It was the only rabbit we ever saw in Africa.

Two rhinos that had started threatening each other in the afternoon were slowly circling the water hole together. We could hear them snorting on the far side. About eleven o'clock one of them appeared below us. Blood was streaming from its left shoulder. The victor had disappeared. He was probably on his honeymoon.

It was nearly midnight. The beautiful, graceful animals had retired for the night. Only the brutes were left, the rhinos, the wild buffalos, and the elephants. For the first time in years as many as sixteen rhinos had been there together. The most ever counted in one evening at Treetops was nineteen.

We crawled into our narrow beds. I eased myself below a branch hoping I would remember not to sit up suddenly in the morning.

On our first visit to Kenya we passed up the new modern

hotel and stayed at the Norfolk on the outskirts of Nairobi. It was the traditional hotel full of atmosphere and built around a courtyard. Several safaris were being assembled there. We wanted to watch them but Charlie and I had to go into the city shopping for the last thing we ever expected to buy in Africa—felt hats. The head of USIS, Ed Stansbury, whom we had met in Saigon four years earlier, had secured an invitation for the three of us to the garden party to be held for Queen Mother Elizabeth the following week. The one dress requirement was that the gentlemen must wear hats.

I do not believe Charlie had ever owned a hat between his baby bonnet and his air force cap. I had thrown my hat away in Khartoum rather than lug it through Africa.

Since hats are not normally sold in Nairobi, the local merchants had imported the discarded stock of London wholesalers—obviously not those catering to Bond Street. We finally selected a couple of natty numbers and put the cost down to the price of admission. Charlie's might have been worn by the Lone Ranger and Buster Keaton would have been delighted with mine.

The next morning our "safari car" called for us with driver, cook, and food. It was a combination station wagon, truck, and jeep known as a Land-Rover. There were two hatches in the top that could be raised for observation or picture taking. Each hatch bore the notation, "Beware of lions in rear." Several days later in what was then called Tanganyika, we learned why.

The first part of our trip was through flat "Mau Mau country" and we passed several "Rehabilitation Camps" for Mau Mau prisoners. Needless to say, we never thought that the leader of the Mau Maus would in a few years be the leader of Kenya; most of the Mau Maus were Kikiyus.

When the countryside became more rolling with a little more vegetation, we were told we were in the land of the Masai tribe and soon we saw some of their warriors.

They had smeared their bodies with red clay, and stained their hair the same color. Their togalike robes left their rear ends bare. Though their ear lobes are pierced, they suspend metal rings six inches in diameter from holes drilled in the tops of their ears.

They grow no crops but have enormous herds of cattle, which they never butcher for meat. They live on milk and blood sucked through straws from their animals' necks. When they have had their fill of blood, the hole in the neck is sealed with mud.

Cattle are a status symbol like Cadillacs at Miami Beach. They are used for purchasing wives, not mistresses. The "dowry" is usually ten to twenty or more.

We visited Tsavo Park on our first trip and Amboselli on our second. We enjoyed every minute in each park but though one never tires of seeing animals roaming wild, reading about them can be tiresome.

We had so much fun watching the animals, I thought that in all fairness some of them should have been at the Queen Mother's garden party.

We returned to Nairobi the night before this unusual event and were sincerely grateful that we had been invited. We were told that no cameras would be allowed, and not wishing to offend anyone or be rude American tourists, we left ours behind. If there were any Englishmen there without cameras, we did not see them.

In describing the party I suppose I should begin with the Lords. Charlie was impeccably dressed in his gray 1956 Rogers Peet and his mandatory, bought-for-the-occasion, fedora. It was obvious that he would not have to worry about sunburn.

I was, of course, immaculate, and wearing a tie that Mary gave me for Christmas with a single, embroidered white mouse—"A mouse may look at a king."

Mary was wearing her dress girdle.

We had a blue sticker for our car and we were supposed to

be in our parking place by three-thirty, although the Queen Mother was not to appear until four-thirty. It was suggested we leave at two forty-five but we left at two-thirty because Mary wanted ringside seats.

We parked on the lawn in front of the long, low, impressive governor's mansion. One terrace was roped off with white ropes and soon became known to us as the "Paddock," as this is where the Queen Mother strolled about later.

We walked across the lawn through gaps in the ropes to the other side, where hundreds of chairs and tables were set up under the trees and in open fields. Beyond were tents where tea, and presumably crumpets, were being served.

Everyone was appropriating chairs from the tables and bringing them over to the lawn under the trees where it was cooler and there was more to be seen. Not that there was not a lot to be seen everywhere! What a sight! We had never seen such a variety of costumes or so many colors. The European women were dressed in anything from the Gay Nineties to the sack. There were quite a number of tall, stoop-shouldered English women of undetermined age, dressed in pale pink or lavender, with parasols to match. One in front of us was wearing a hat that looked like a marshmallow. On the whole, though, we thought them smartly dressed, particularly for a place where the stores can provide so little.

The Indian women had draped themselves in some of the most beautiful saris we had ever seen—brilliant greens, scarlets, yellows, purples, etc., overlaid with gold.

There were many African women mingling in the crowd. Some wore the latest European fashions, but most were in cheap cotton prints. A few had simply wrapped themselves in a length of bright-colored cloth. Many had brought very young babies with them and thought nothing of nursing them in public.

The men were as interesting as the women. Some of the

English wore gray top hats; others badly beaten felts just out of moth balls. A number carried shooting sticks and there were a number of tightly rolled black umbrellas. After all, the rains would begin in six weeks!

The various army uniforms were just as fascinating—from the plaid trousers and kilts of the Scotch, to the jauntily feathered hats of the Australians and New Zealanders. Most of the Indian men were dressed in European clothes, but the bearded Sikhs wore turbans—usually white but often blue or pink.

The African men's clothes were the most fantastic. To describe just one of many: he had a turban colored halfway between bright purple and shocking pink. Over his shoulder was a bright orange scarf. This was worn over an ordinary blue serge pin-striped European-cut jacket. Below this was a white skirt extending just below his knees. There were several inches of brown calves and then light blue cotton socks. He wore light tan high-laced shoes. He was quite a sight but there were hundreds just as astonishing.

We were early enough to get some chairs and put them in a good spot under a tree. For late arrivals, there were none. Then began the game of "There she is." It was a kind of "musical chairs." The rules were quite simple and we soon caught on: those without chairs suddenly shouted "There She Is." Those with chairs would spring to their feet and rush to see the Queen Mother. When they returned from the false alarm their chairs were gone.

For the first hour or so the fight for chairs was fairly good-natured. Then many of the women became desperate and nasty.

Once I was standing about two inches in front of my chair. I heard a noise and started to sit down quickly. Only superb balance and quick reflexes kept me from sitting in the lap of a dowager who had appropriated my chair—literally behind my back.

We went to the paddock right by the gate where the Queen Mother came out. We three were in the front row. Then the Queen Mother appeared and suddenly Charlie and I were six rows back. If only the Yale line could charge like English women at the sight of royalty!

An aisle was cleared and Charlie and I looked over the heads of the crowd. We were not too surprised to find Mary in the front row on the other side. We were not prepared for her curtsy as the Queen Mother walked by. The latter was wearing a "Mother of the Bride" costume the color of melted peach ice cream.

Before leaving the paddock the Queen Mother spoke to about a hundred and fifty persons who were presented to her. The most interesting of these were the tribal chiefs. Most of them wore animal skins or feathers, often in combination with modern dress.

The party was completely integrated and everyone was in a holiday mood. We decided that in 1959 the institution of the Royal garden party was doing more to hold the Commonwealth together than the British Navy.

3

"Here the World Is Still Young and Fragile"

TANZANIA was known as Tanganyika on both our trips to that country. There were very few formalities on crossing the border from Kenya. We entered the country each time at the same place and motored to Arusha through the land of the Meru tribe. Unlike the Masai, they do a good deal of farming, growing among other things coffee and corn. The latter, after harvesting, they hang in bags from trees to outwit the numerous rats.

We saw giraffes everywhere. Not just in the game reserves, but along the sides of the roads, in the fields, silhouetted against the sky and sometimes running stiff-legged right in front of our Land-Rover.

You can usually spot them from a distance, as their necks and heads tower above the surrounding greenery. Their favorite food is the leaf of the acacia tree. The latter are flat-topped and I often wondered if that were due to giraffes nibbling anything their mouths could reach. They seldom eat low-growing vegetation because it is almost inaccessible to them. They have no knees in their front legs, which they must spread far apart if their long necks are to reach the ground. Their tough upper lips separate the acacia leaves from the even more numerous acacia thorns.*

As one approaches Arusha the land becomes hilly and more cultivated. In the distance is Mt. Meru—14,000 feet.

On our first trip we passed three men with their black faces painted with white streaks. When we tried to photograph them, two ran into the bushes and the third lay down on the ground and covered himself with his robe.

Outside the Arusha Hotel is a large sign saying it is exactly halfway from Cairo to the Cape and the exact center of Kenya, Tanganyika, and Uganda.

Mary, Charlie, and I spent two nights in Arusha, one going to and one returning from the Ngorongoro Crater. We visited the marketplace but left our cameras behind. In 1959 they scared people and we were warned against taking pictures, particularly of women.

Mary fascinated the latter with the pop-it beads she had brought from New York. She took the large string she wore around her neck for the occasion and broke it into half a dozen bracelets for women and children. They were surprised and pleased. She took a reserve supply from her purse and made more friends. Charlie and I gave the kids hard candies and balloons that whistled when the air escaped. Little black girls howled with laughter when we gave them tiny, white, naked celluloid dolls.

The people were gay and friendly and acted as though the circus had come to town. Then Mary made a ten-strike. She persuaded one of the native women to sell her two of her

---

* What we at first thought were haystacks in the fields and along the roadside turned out to be giant anthills four to eight feet high and reddish brown in color.

necklaces she was wearing. They could not be bought in stores or markets.

Each necklace was made of ten or twelve concentric circles of colored beads strung on round loops of stiff wire. The loops were fixed rigidly together, making a flat, not limp, necklace about an inch wide.

The woman was wearing four of these, the inside ring of one necklace just a little larger than the outside ring of the smaller one. The necklaces together made a band of colored beads four inches wide sticking out stiffly from her neck.

Mary put her two necklaces around her neck (carefully over a scarf) much to the delight of all the people. Then she and the woman did a mock native dance together. The crowd loved it.

On our way from Arusha to Ngorongoro Crater we were stopped at a checkpoint while two boys with nets searched our Land-Rover for the deadly tsetse fly. The altitude of the crater's rim is too high for them to fly over but they could be carried over in a vehicle. They are easy to identify by their wings, which fold back close to their bodies like modern fighter planes.

The boys caught three tsetse flies. They are feared because their bite often, but not always, gives human beings sleeping sickness. I was particularly concerned as my younger brother Jack died of that disease in 1928.

We climbed for an hour or so and stopped on the crest of a narrow ridge for an amazing sight. Behind us we could see the Great Rift. It is a deep gash in the earth several miles wide which extends from the Red Sea southwest for more than a thousand miles across Africa. The skeletons of some of the earliest men have been excavated from the soil of the rift.

Ahead of us the ground dropped away to the floor of the Ngorongoro Crater two thousand feet below. We knew it to be the remains of an extinct volcano and expected it to be rough and rocky and rather small. Instead, we saw a great green bowl flat at the bottom with steep sides equally lush. We could see a large lake and were told that nearby was a salt lick. What we thought were the shadows of passing clouds soon were revealed to us as herds of pasturing wild animals whose ancestors had been down there for centuries.

We drove along the crest of the ridge for about five miles to the Ngorongoro Crater Camp. There were about a dozen thatched roof huts. Most were of logs, but ours was made of hand-hewn boards.

Inside there was a tiny living room with a cheerful fire burning in the stone fireplace. There was a small bedroom for Mary and me, and a tiny room for Charlie. There was a bathroom with dirty running water in the tub, a basin and pitcher on a dresser, but no toilet. We did have an elegant bamboo outhouse. There was also a small dining room and a kitchen with a wood-burning stove.

We poured Scotch and sodas and sat on the doorstep and watched the sun go down. Since the crater is a surprising ten miles in diameter, it took some time for the inky shadow of night to glide over the green carpet far below us. It was quiet and peaceful except for the strange evening noises of dozens of different kinds of birds. We were entranced and therefore silent.

Our mood was broken when dinner was announced by our traveling cook, whose name sounded like "Sue-Jenny." What a strange sight in the wilderness. On his head was a white chef's hat. His scarlet robe stopped just short enough of the floor to reveal two very large black bare feet. His chicken dinner by lamplight was delicious.

It was cold that night and chilly when Sue-Jenny brought us the inevitable tea at 6:30 A.M. An hour later we started down into the crater in our Land-Rover. We had not gone far before sighting a dozen wild buffalo in a field to our right. The ranger with us explained why they are considered the most dangerous of the "big five" (elephants, rhinos, lions, leopards, and buffalo). They are the only ones that are good eating, and also their skins are valuable. As a result, they are the special prey of poachers and therefore have learned to hate men.

Ten minutes later a leopard bounded across the road right in front of us and then glowered at us from the underbrush thirty yards to our left. We were fortunate to see him, as most people who go to Africa never see a leopard.

A few miles farther on Charlie spotted another leopard as we rounded a corner. We could just see his head in the tall grass between two bushes. We took quick pictures and then I quietly raised the overhead hatch to try to get a better shot while Mary and Charlie watched him. When I got the hatch up he had suddenly disappeared. One moment he was there. The next moment he was gone without a sound or a ripple in the grass.

I started to look around from the vantage point of the hatch opening, hoping to get another glimpse of the leopard. The ranger pulled me down and slammed the hatch. He explained leopards often circled around and sprang suddenly from the bushes or out of a tree. Now we understood the reason for the sign on the hatch, "Beware of lions in rear."

The trip down into the crater was interesting. There were myriad wild flowers, but yellow ones predominated. They covered the ground and grew up into the trees—apparently some sort of vine. Wild lilies were everywhere. About half-way down we went through a forest of strangely shaped trees. They were forty to fifty feet high with foliage only at the top—which was flat. Finally we came out on the last open slopes just above the crater floor. Half a mile away we spied a lone rhino. We took off across country in our Land-Rover and snapped a couple of quick pictures from fifty yards with the sun in a bad position. Then we circled to within twenty yards with the sun at our back. I pressed the button of my 3-D camera. Nothing happened. What a time to be out of film!

We hardly breathed as I put in a new one. I pressed the button. Again nothing. I tried again. Another failure. I opened the camera—tried everything, no success. I had come thousands of miles to see these animals but I also wanted to photograph them. I was even more frustrated, half an hour later, when we drove close to a pair of lions dozing in the sun. The male stretched himself, roused his female and they mated, oblivious of their audience. Maybe they knew my camera was not working.

Some years later Mary's brother and nephew had a similar experience, but have pictures to prove it. They also learned that when lions are in the mood, they mate every twenty minutes for the better part of twenty-four hours.

Although there are a few rutted paths in the crater, the surface is generally hard and you can drive anywhere. There were two other safari wagons in the crater that day but we seldom saw them.

All around us were herds of animals. There were gnus by the hundreds. The buffalo on our western plains must have been like this a hundred years or more ago. They are dark animals with horns and beards. Their legs are longer than those of buffalo. They look like a cross between a deer and a buffalo.

On the edges of each herd of gnus hovered a few hyenas. They seldom kill anything for themselves. They share in the kill made by other animals. They follow pregnant animals and devour the babies at the moment of birth.

Gazelles were everywhere—the larger Grant gazelles and the smaller Thomson gazelles. The latter are the most appealing animals I have ever seen. They are small, graceful and quick, with soft, curious eyes. I would have liked to have one for a pet. Better still, if there is such a thing as reincarnation, I want to come back as a Thomson gazelle.

As plentiful as the gnus and gazelles were the zebras. We understood why, as half the latter were obviously pregnant. We had a picnic lunch in the only grove of trees in the crater. Nearby were the ruins of a house of a German farmer who had lived alone in this fantastic place before World War I. He left when Tanganyika was taken away from Germany as part of the peace treaty.

Only here were we permitted to leave our Land-Rover. There were no wild animals nearby but plenty of storks and cranes strolling nonchalantly—too proud to acknowledge our presence.

After luncheon we resumed our leisurely circumnavigation of the crater. Though we saw many of the same kinds of animals, their groupings, surroundings, and lighting were different and therefore new.

We reluctantly turned from the crater floor at four o'clock and started the long climb to the rim over a road that seemed more miserable on the way up than we had remembered it on the way down. Suddenly we discovered that we were tired and bone-weary from hours of standing up in our jolting and bouncing, practically springless safari wagon. We had been too absorbed in the animals to risk missing anything by sitting down.

We did not find much relaxation on the hard seats on the three-hour trip up. We were glad to see a wood fire burning under the tank outside our cabin. There was enough hot water for each of us to relax in the enormous tin tub before another delicious dinner prepared by Sue-Jenny.

In the morning we returned to Arusha for lunch, passing many giraffes on the way. They still interested us but the giant anthills had lost their novelty.

That afternoon we stopped at Moshi to see the Council Hall of the Chaga tribe. It was a new building whose interior was reminiscent of a small New England church. Here the chiefs representing each subsection of the tribe met for their deliberations, presided over by the paramount chief, Tom Marealle.

We motored on to our hotel in Marangu at the foot of Mount Kilimanjaro to clean up and change before returning to Moshi for dinner with Chief Tom. We found him an unusual man, well educated, traveled and wise.

After cocktails on his broad veranda we had a delicious Tanganyika dinner. First we had green bananas in a heavy gravy. This was followed by a spicy rice dish with cloves and meat. After several more courses that we could not identify, we finished with a really fine banana soufflé. The other guests were an interesting group of Africans, Indians and Europeans—some in business and some in government.

We arose early the next morning, Thursday, February 5, 1959, to see Mount Kilimanjaro at dawn. It is frequently hidden by clouds all day, often for weeks at a time, but we were fortunate. There was not a cloud in the sky. The rising sun tinted the twin snow-capped peaks not with the traditional pink, but with a vibrant gold-washed salmon.

It was a beautiful sight but not what we had anticipated. The travel folder pictures had led us to expect one mountain shaped like Fujiyama with the crown sliced off. Instead, Kilimanjaro has twin peaks, the flat-topped extinct volcano Kibo and another pointed one that appeared almost as high.

In spite of its beauty we were a little disappointed and tried to explain to each other why we all reacted the same way to the tallest mountain in Africa, nineteen thousand feet.

Five years later Mary and I saw Kilimanjaro from the Amboselli game reserve. Not even the travel folders had prepared us for its beauty from that angle.

Maybe my appreciation was enhanced by the fact that instead of being roused at dawn to dress and go out to see it as at Marangu, I had a civilized view from my bed.

Seeing only the one peak made the mountain look higher. There was nothing nearby to detract from its majesty. The snow was so smooth that it looked like a giant birthday cake. On the right side was an extra fold of luscious white icing.

On this second trip we returned to Arusha, where Tom Marealle joined us for luncheon. We had been in sporadic correspondence with him for five years and had arranged our meeting ahead of time. We found him just as attractive and knowledgeable as we remembered.

This time we did not bypass Manyara on our trip to the Ngorongoro Crater and we were glad we did not. We turned left before going through the tsetse fly checkpoint and motored to the Manyara Lodge. We arrived at the same time as a delegation from Red China. Schoolgirls were lined up to give them flowers. The Communist Chinese were all over Africa in 1964, and particularly so in what was then Tanganyika. After their coup in Zanzibar they were instrumental in bringing about the merger of the two countries into Tanzania.

One glance at the uniforms and business suits of the Chinese dignitaries led us to believe that all the good Chinese tailors must have moved to Hong Kong. One of the few bonds remaining between the Russian and Chinese "Red brothers" is their ill-fitting clothes.

At Manyara Lodge we had three adjoining cabins, one each for the Fleischmanns, Haneses, and Lords. Only a ten-foot border of flowers separated us from the rim of the Great Rift. A thousand feet below, we could see Lake Manyara and the fields and trees near it. It was an oasis in the dry, drab rift.

The lodge was so modern that besides a beautiful swimming pool there were picture windows in the bathrooms of the individual cabins. It is an unusual experience to luxuriate in chest-deep hot water at sunset and watch a bull elephant browse his way across a clearing below you.

The next morning, the six of us started down to Lake Manyara in our two Land-Rovers. Though there were two hatches in the roof of each, there was no seat under the afterhatch. I borrowed a heavy iron porch furniture chair on which to sit during the long trip down and back.

In less than an hour we were on the floor of the rift. Much as we enjoyed seeing elephants, buffalo, baboons, etc., all around us, we had come primarily to see lions—not on the ground or mating, but in trees! Only in Manyara does one see them there. The explanation we were given was that the climate was so hot in the Great Rift that lions climbed up into the trees for comfort.

I was watching several frolicking baboons when our Land-Rover stopped under a large tree. I looked up. There was a lion stretched out on every branch. I counted nine, some almost within reach.

One big lioness got up and crept along a huge branch that extended two feet over my hatch. I remembered the legend and tradition that I had nothing to worry about. I also thought that it was probably better not to move. Fortunately our driver had different ideas. Our car shot forward suddenly and I tumbled backward along with the heavy iron chair. I did not realize I had been hurt until several hours later when someone in our party asked about the bruise and discoloration on my right arm.

We saw more lions in trees, including one so pregnant Mary wanted to wait to take some unusual pictures.

After lunch we motored thirty miles to the Ngorongoro Crater. On the way, we gave a lift to an English girl and a heavily bearded Frenchman who were roaming Africa without a tent or benefit of clergy.

They took their sleeping bag and left us just before we arrived at the Ngorongoro Crater Camp. It had changed a lot in five years. We had not brought our own food or cook. Instead there was an attractive dining room separated from the bar by an enormous fireplace. The warmth from the blazing logs was welcome at sundown at eight thousand feet.

There were only a few more cabins than on our previous visit. They were smaller because they had no dining rooms or kitchens, but the rooms were larger and ours included, besides our two beds, an armchair. I was glad for the latter.

It is strange how long it sometimes takes before you become aware of an injury. I had not known about my bruised arm until one of our group called my attention to it.

I was not aware of the pain in my rib until I went to bed that night. After a few hours I found it more comfortable to sit up in the chair. In this position, I could doze fitfully. In Mombasa, ten days later, a doctor told me I was recovering from a cracked rib.

A new road had been cut to the floor of the crater and the descent took only half an hour. The road was extremely rough and not recommended for anyone with a bad rib.

Because of heavy rains nearly a third of the crater was covered with water whereas in our previous visit the lake had been small. The contraction in the land area had crowded the thousands of animals into smaller grazing grounds. They surrounded us on all sides. Though gnus, zebras and gazelles were the most plentiful, there were many harte-beests and topi. Scavenging nearby were the inevitable hyenas and jackals.

We left the flat plain and headed for the underbrush in the foothills. Crashing and bumbling along we twice came upon a rhino with a young baby and stopped to watch them pass. We recalled the expression, "the baby had a face that only a mother could love."

Soon we saw two lionesses with a young one near a grass-lined gully. We watched them pad down the bank to drink from the stream at the bottom. Then the three of them stretched in the sun and went to sleep.

We followed the gully for a quarter of a mile and then spotted the kill. It was a wildebeest that must have been dead only a very short time as only a very little of it had been eaten.

On our side of the little stream, about fifty vultures waited a hundred yards away from the carcass. On the other bank were two more groups silently waiting. Then one more courageous vulture near us took a few steps forward. He was followed by two more. The rest remained motionless.

In five minutes the leader was on the dead gnu and four

or five of his apprehensive followers only a few feet away. Some of the vultures on the opposite bank edged forward.

Soon there were half a dozen birds feasting for a change instead of picking bare bones. We wondered why the other vultures held back.

Soon we saw the reason for their timidity. Suddenly a lioness appeared dashing at great speed toward the kill and the predatory birds. They left in a hurry. We could almost hear the cautious birds saying, "We told you so."

The lioness was not going to allow any animal not in her pride of lions to dine on what she had killed for the family.

We spent that night back on the rim of the crater. Instead of returning by the way we had come through Arusha, as on our first trip, we motored across the Serengeti Plain to the Seronera Lodge.

One of the fascinating facets of animal-viewing in East Africa is the variety of conditions and surroundings in which they are seen.

Treetops is unique. There is nothing like it anywhere else in the world. The tree house may be artificial and twentieth century but the animals are genuine and their way of life ageless and unchanging. And where else can you see them at night?

No man has ever conceived of a zoo ten miles in diameter with the walls of an extinct volcano as the only restraining barrier for thousands and thousands and thousands of animals—some graceful and pretty—others ugly and impressive: the Ngorongoro Crater.

Then there is Manyara in the Great Rift where mankind may have been born and lions sleep in trees.

But to have some understanding of what Africa must have been like before Stanley and Livingstone, one must cross the Serengeti Plain.

Nothing we had read or seen had prepared us for this experience. After an hour's motoring we had dropped the rim of the crater behind us. Our horizon was caused by the curvature of the earth. It was like being at sea. The illusion was strengthened by the billowing green grass extending for miles with the myriad white wildflowers looking like whitecaps. To our left, miles away, we could barely distinguish a few shadowy outlines against the sky. Were they mirages or mountain peaks thrust above the sea by volcanic action?

The seaborne illusion faded reluctantly. It was not waves but animals that gave motion to the landscape. They were everywhere in uncountable numbers. We guessed that we could see at least fifty thousand at a time. But maybe one hundred thousand would have been more correct. (Early the next morning the head ranger flew Mary south in his two-seater plane to see the annual great migration of animals. He estimated the closely packed wildebeests at three hundred thousand and a herd of zebras at fifty thousand.)

I had seen so many of the larger animals that I instinctively focused my attention on the little Thomson gazelles. They have the grace of ballet dancers and the personality of your first three-year-old granddaughter. It is as though they had been created through a merger of God and Walt Disney.

A black stripe separates their white bellies from their beautiful suntan bodies. Their tiny ears perked up beneath their short V-shaped horns augment the impression of curiosity in their childlike eyes. Their black tails never stop waving in a gesture which is obviously friendly. Then, the novelty of mankind having worn off, they dash away like Donder and Blitzen.

At about one o'clock we approached a small lake with a pink peninsula extending from the near shore. We thought it an ideal place for our picnic. It was a nice place for lunch but our peninsula left just before we arrived. It was composed of tens of thousands of pink flamingoes standing packed together in the shallow water. As they darkened the sky over our heads we could see that the underside of their wings was almost red.

About four o'clock that afternoon, in a part of the plain where there were a few sparse trees and some underbrush, our driver exclaimed, "Cheetah."

There he was, a blur twenty yards to our left. He looked like a leopard to me. We took off after him. We bounced and jolted across country and ran right over small bushes in our pursuit. I looked at the speedometer. It registered eighty kilometers, or fifty miles an hour, and we were just barely able to keep pace with the cheetah.

I took some jolting movies out the window but when the driver stopped so I could take better ones, the animal far outdistanced us.

Then we spotted two cheetahs running in the opposite direction. In an instant we were off in pursuit again. They are so graceful and quick, they seem to glide rather than run. We raced side by side for a while until we lost them in the underbrush.

As at Ngorongoro Crater Lodge five years earlier, we had brought our own food. Mary, Dorette Fleischmann and DeWitt Hanes planned the menus for our two days at the Seronera Lodge but the meals were cooked by the servants who lived there.

After Mary returned from her early morning flight south to see the migration, we started out in our two Land-Rovers, looking for the most elusive of all animals, leopards. No success.

We soon got over our disappointment. In the tall grass near a little stream we saw the heads of several lions. A hundred yards away on the plains stood a topi, obviously suspicious and alert. Standing up with our heads out of the hatches of the two Land-Rovers, we counted a pride of twenty-one lions in the tall grass. There were nine lionesses and twelve cubs. There was no male in sight.

From our high perch we could see the ambush but the lions must have been hidden from the sight of the topi. They were spread out in a skirmish line a quarter of a mile long—poised for the kill.

Our sympathies were with the topi and we (not the driver) were prepared to blow the horn to warn him if necessary. He would take a few cautious steps toward the concealed lions and then hesitate, smell the air and stand transfixed.

Meanwhile the lions were creeping toward him, stalking him through the grass, which never moved with their passage. We could see every movement from our elevated vantage point.

When it appeared that the topi would not come within range of the lions' swift surprise attack, two lionesses rather obviously ran off in the opposite direction, as though to allay his suspicions and lure him into the ambush.

He was too smart to advance but neither did he retreat. When we asked our driver why the topi did not run away, he said that he was on guard to warn the other animals of the presence of the lions. It seemed like a good explanation except there were no other animals in sight. Maybe the other animals were smarter and our topi should have spelled his name with a "D."

That afternoon we were excited at seeing a leopard in the fork of a dead tree. Usually they are hidden by leaves or underbrush. When they run there is little time for observation, and less for pictures. This one glared at us for five minutes and then leisurely descended the tree and slunk away into the forest.

On our way back to the Seronera Lodge we were a little sad. None of us had any plans to return to Africa. We had learned to love the animals and knew we would miss them and remember them with nostalgia as one vaguely recalls kindergarten playmates.

The gazelles had been lovable, the baboons amusing, and most of the others, fascinating. But we never expected to see animals gay.

Our last evening we did.

We veered right toward a clump of trees that looked like an oasis in the flat grasslands through which we had been motoring. The semidarkness of the leaf-filtered sunlight confused our vision. Then we saw them! Forty or fifty impalas were frolicking in this cool and shaded playground. They hardly seemed to touch the earth. They were not jumping or leaping so much as soaring. They seemed to float effortlessly through space, descending every fifteen or twenty feet to make brief contact with the ground. Each one seemed carried away with its own exuberance and joy. It was as though Peter Pan had been reincarnated many times. The spontaneity of their happiness had the supreme attribute of innocence.

The Garden of Eden must have been like this before the curse of man and woman had brought guilt into the world. As I reveled in the enjoyment of the scene before me, the heritage of Adam and Eve, Cain and Abel, asserted itself. I felt a twinge of conscience. Was I being disloyal to the Thomson gazelles?

The next morning we flew back to Nairobi in two small chartered planes rather than spend three days reversing our fishhook-shaped trail through Kenya and Tanzania.

The sign at the dirt strip on the Serengeti Plain that served as an airport read:

"Here the world is still young and fragile. Held in trust for your sons and ours."

4

Hippos Keep Their Promises

ON OUR first trip to Africa we flew from Nairobi to Usumbura in the Belgian Congo and motored from there to Bukavu along the shore of Lake Tanganyika. We were surprised to see good-sized steamers on the lake. We learned that it was 480 miles long, and that the ships were brought in in sections and assembled on the lake shore. No one swims in Lake Tanganyika because it is filled with bilharzia, the tiny parasite that can enter any orifice in the body with disastrous results.

We struck across country from Lake Tanganyika to Lake Kivu and spent the night in Bukavu. Years later we were glad that we were not there to witness the massacres of civilians and soldiers alike as the tribes wreaked vengeance on each other. It was in Bukavu that the mercenaries held out in 1967 demanding safe passage out of the country.

We remember it as an attractive small town built on flower-laden hills that sloped down to peaceful blue waters.

From Bukavu we motored to Albert National Park spending a night at Goma on the way. When the chief game warden warned us not to leave our thatched cabins at night because of the animals, we thought he was trying to impress us as tourists. The next morning at sunrise our cabin was surrounded by a herd of wild buffalo.

That morning the warden took us out personally so that we could go to parts of the park not usually seen by visitors. We saw so many hippos that he was prompted to tell us the natives' legend about them.

"God created hippos to live on land in Africa. They found it so hot that they went back to God to ask if they could go in the water to cool off. He said He was afraid they would eat the fish. The hippos promised not to if they were allowed to go in the water. They would only eat on land.

"Hippos have a way of every now and then raising their heads out of the water, giving a great snort and opening their mouths very wide. The natives say the snort is to call God's attention and then they open their mouths wide to show there are no fish bones in their throats!"

The next day we started out for Butembo. About five o'clock we stopped for tea, beer and, most important of all, gasoline. We were heading into desolate country.

There were only a few widely scattered thatched native huts. As the sun set, we could hear the jungle noises. Just as we approached the top of a hill the car stopped. The gas gauge showed empty and we found the reason. The connecting gas line between the tank and the engine had come apart.

It looked like an unpleasant situation, with our having to spend a foodless night in the jungle wilderness.

Leaving Charlie in the car with Mary, our driver-interpreter, Mr. Jolly, and I started to walk ahead down the road.

We didn't know what to expect or to hope for, but there was no use sitting idly by in the broken-down car.

Around the first bend in the road we were surprised and delighted to see several lights and the outline of a European house half a mile away. It was the first one we had seen in more than two hours. It turned out to be a small Seventh Day Adventist Mission. Four men, two women and several children were having dinner, which included corn on the cob from their own garden.

When we told them of our plight, one man and a boy put five gallons of gas in a can and drove us back to our car. Needless to say, Mary and Charlie were glad to see us. It was pitch black by then. They were not too pleased with their situation and wondered what had happened to Mr. Jolly and me.

There was still the question of the broken gas connection. Mr. Jolly crawled under the car and forced the two ends together. We had no way of fastening them and they might come apart with any jolt.

The missionaries urged us to spend the night and warned us of the hardships and dangers of trying to go farther before morning. Nevertheless we decided to push on. It was a nerve-wracking ride. We watched the speedometer and made notes so we'd know whether to go forward, backward, or stay put in case of trouble.

We crept along slowly so as to minimize the danger of a bump disrupting our patched gas line. After what seemed an hour, we saw a light in the distance to our right. We dutifully noted the distance covered—seven kilometers, less than five miles! We had been told by the missionaries that we had forty kilometers to go to get to Butembo.

We saw no more signs of habitation except a few thatched huts. Occasionally our headlights would be reflected from eyeballs peering at us from the jungle—natives we hoped, even if hostile. At times we heard the low murmur of disembodied voices.

We were relieved when the speedometer showed we had done twenty kilometers, halfway. If we broke down again, at least we could walk forward, not backward. But we did not have to. We crept into Butembo at nine o'clock.

Somewhere on this slow cautious ride we crossed the equator again.

Anything would have been better than a night in the car, but we didn't have to settle for "anything." Our hotel was very attractive and we had our own cabin with hot water and roses on the roof. The martinis were almost as good as the delicious dinner.

We felt like stowaways on a raft who hoped to be picked up by a fishing boat but instead find themselves on a Greek shipping magnate's yacht.

The next day, Friday the thirteenth, was without incident. We motored to Mutwanga, at the foot of "the Mountains of the Moon." Though they are on the equator, we could see glaciers, and snow on the highest peaks.

The following day we crossed into Uganda and had lunch in Elizabeth Park. This park adjoins Albert Park in the Congo so that the animals have an enormous preserve over which to roam. They don't know the difference between the Belgian and English flags.

At three o'clock we started out in a launch on the narrow Kazinga Channel that connects Lake Edward with Lake Albert. We saw hundreds of birds and dozens of hippos and one forked-tongue lizard so large that he looked like a dragon. What we had really come to see were elephants.

Finally we had our reward. Across the water on a hillside, we saw several large ones. We approached the other bank, shut off the motor and drifted, talking in whispers at first, then not at all. Coming cautiously down the hillside in single file were fourteen elephants, including half a dozen babies, two of them very small. At their head was a very big bull with enormous tusks. He would advance a few feet and the whole line would follow. When he stopped, they all stopped. Apparently he smelled humans and was suspicious. Elephants have poor eyesight but keen noses.

The wind was blowing down the river slightly toward the bank. The elephants were coming down a path diagonally toward the water. When they got downwind of us, the leader would stop. Then we would drift a little way so the leader would not smell us. The line of elephants would move forward a few yards.

We held our breaths. They were getting nearer and nearer. What a sight! Mary clicked her camera. They all stopped. The leader raised his trunk and spread his ears. Finally they came on again.

"Time is up." It was the launch pilot speaking. He started his engine and headed for home. We could have cried. In five minutes the elephants would have been in the water.

It is common knowledge that the best time to see animals is at sundown (or sunrise). In the Belgian Congo that is the time you go out. Since Uganda was British, the schedule was set up to get you back in time for tea!

When we got back to the lodge we were so annoyed we passed up the British drink and took a Scotch one instead. We were very disappointed. We had been told that Elizabeth Park was really the place to see elephants and we thought we had been thwarted.

We were wrong. It was about six miles to the park exit, but Mr. Jolly took us by a longer route. Soon we saw elephants by threes and fours, then eights and tens.

We passed a thicket and on our right were a dozen elephants not fifty yards away. We stopped to take pictures. Just as I was about to press the button, the car shot forward. I remonstrated for a second, but Mr. Jolly told me the big lead elephant was about to charge. They are so fast (over a

short distance) that they can reach you and push over your
car before you can pick up speed. Mr. Jolly said he always
kept his car in gear when he stopped near elephants.

We counted 185 elephants in 20 minutes. Then, after
we left the park, we were held up for twenty-five minutes
by two enormous bull elephants who blocked our road while
a score of others, including some very young babies, took
their food-picking time crossing over. We would have
stopped even if there had not been signs, "Elephants have
the right of way."

The next morning we motored to Mt. Hoyo through
jungles that looked as Africa was supposed to look. Whole
hillsides were covered with immense ferns. Trees seventy-
five to a hundred feet high were commonplace—many trail-
ing vines from their topmost branches. Some of the trees
had flowers. Red, white and orange were the most common
colors. We could smell the jungle all around us.

After luncheon we visited a lovely waterfall nearby and
then were shown one of twenty recently discovered caves.
One was enough. As far as I was concerned, a cave is a cave
is a cave.

That evening we returned to the cave to see some native
dancing. Although there was a touch of Broadway in the
staging, the dancers were authentic and fascinating.

About fifteen of us sat on a long wooden bench. The cave
was lighted only by two ultraviolet lamps on the ground—
right in front of us. It was so dark we could hardly distinguish the black bodies of the dancers. The men wore red
turbans, white diapers and white beaded anklets. The girls
had orange turbans, "fish-net" bras, and eight-inch squares
of yellow cloth fore and aft at the waist. They also wore
white beaded anklets. All of their costumes had been treated
so as to glow in the ultraviolet light. As they danced in the
darkness their naked black bodies were almost impercepti-
ble. They looked like disembodied spirits. The music of

the drums soon had our feet tapping to the marvelous rhythm.

Each dance got better. The last one was fantastic. The dancers had worked themselves into an ecstasy. The music was very soft and you could hear the slap, slap of bare feet on the packed earth.

When the performance was over, lights were turned on and we got our first look at the performers. They were all young and some of the girls strikingly beautiful. They lined up so we could take a picture. Then they motioned for us to wait a moment. The girls wanted to remove their bras. Maybe "Toplessness" started here.

When they were ready I aimed my camera and snapped. Nothing! Out of film.

The following morning we went to see pygmies in their village half a mile away. It was an olfactory experience I would not want to repeat often. Pygmies do not bathe from the cradle to the grave. Even though we saw them only outdoors, the three of us were afraid we were going to be violently ill. Fortunately, Mary had a stick of concentrated perfume that we rubbed on our upper lips from time to time.

Pygmies live in family groups. They stay in one place for a few months and then move on. Every two years they return to where they were before. Each group builds its own village, usually close to the site of one that has been abandoned but never on the same spot.

If a pygmy wishes to marry a girl from another family group or clan, one of his sisters or a female cousin must marry his wife's brother or male cousin. If he wants to get rid of his wife and give her back to her own clan, he can not do so unless the other couple agrees to split up also.

This system would sure complicate things in Hollywood.

Most pygmies are under four feet in height and rather repulsive-looking. They have no bridges in their noses, which lie flat on their faces. They are the most cheerful and unspoiled natives in Africa, laughing and frolicking all the time. They are great hunters and will attack anything. They catch antelopes in nets. Even four- and five-year-olds carry bows and arrows and their aim is incredible.

The pygmies danced for us and gave us an exhibition of tree climbing that was amazing. I've been watching for them ever since on the Ed Sullivan Show.

We motored on to Epilu for the night, where we saw the only *African* elephants ever trained to work for man. It had always been thought that, unlike Indian elephants, they could not be domesticated. A Captain Medina (part African, part Portuguese) had succeeded in doing so.

He showed them off but it depressed us. We remembered the herd we had seen coming down to the river.

Captain Medina was the first to capture and ship to zoos an animal called the okapi. They are known as "forest giraffes" and look a little like horses except that their hindquarters are striped like zebras and their necks are very long.

We were up early the next day for a trip of 285 miles over extremely rough roads to Stanleyville. The governor there phoned and asked us over for cocktails at six. He had a beautiful residence with a swimming pool on the bank of the Congo.

The following day we boarded a steamer on the river for a three-day trip to Coquilhatville, a distance of a thousand kilometers.

Our steamer was small but surprisingly comfortable. We had two staterooms in the bow but the view ahead was obstructed as we were pushing two loaded barges and an ancient steamer, the *Wagenia*. The latter looked like a two-story floating tenement. It was crowded with Africans who cooked their own meals on board. In the afternoons they hung their laundry on the railings.

On our steamer the top deck was reserved for the crew and their families, the third deck for second class and the deck in between for first class. We had about thirty fellow passengers of all colors and nationalities with us in the latter.

The lounge and bar aft were cool and attractive and extended nearly the full width of the ship. The wide doors that opened on the narrow decks were always swung back. Sometimes as we slipped between islands or an island and the shore, the foliage scraped both sides of the boat and we had the illusion that we were deep in the jungle.

There were very few bugs or insects but most of them seemed to find their way into the food, which was cooked by the captain's wife. The food in Africa in 1959 was so poor that we all lost weight. Mary talked of borrowing my suspenders to hold up her girdle.

The river was not as wide as we expected, and was dotted with islands. The channel wandered back and forth from shore to shore. We were usually within one hundred yards of the jungle, which came right to the water's edge. The channel was marked with buoys and with boards nailed to trees. The boat navigated from buoy to buoy and from tree to tree.

The jungle was very dense and very beautiful. The trees were of all sizes and shapes—dark and light green and occasionally white and often the shore was thick with pines. From time to time brilliant red, yellow and purple flowers could be seen in the trees or along the banks.

With the exception of a few towns scattered along the water's edge, the only signs of civilization were the villages of some of Africa's most primitive tribes. They were nothing more than little groups of small huts in small clearings in the jungle.

As our boat approached, many boys and women of the villages swam or paddled out to it. The young boys hung on to the side of the steamer begging for cigarettes or swam for bottles thrown overboard. The women in their finest tied their dugout canoes to the barges ahead of us and scrambled on board. They sold fresh fruit and fish. Some sales were made to our steward but most to the Africans. The latter bought not only for their own consumption but to sell for higher prices in the larger cities like Coquilhatville and Léopoldville. In this way they frequently financed their passage.

Often by the time the haggling over prices had been completed the sellers were miles below their villages. They seemed unconcerned about the long paddle back. After all, there was only one boat a week each way and it broke the monotony of their uneventful lives.

I contrasted this experience with my trip in 1927 down the Irrawaddy River in Burma from Mandalay to Prome. Instead of the towering trees of the Congo, the Irrawaddy was lined with low scrub growth. In Burma there was a great deal of river life, on the Congo almost none. I recalled the huge teak rafts with whole families living on board in thatched huts. Many of the rafts were loaded with pottery on the way to market.

On the Congo when we made our few calls at small villages we tied up at conventional docks. Not so on the Irrawaddy. On the latter river there were no scheduled stops. On a signal from the shore, or if there were supplies on board for a native village, a teen-age boy swam ashore with a cord tied around his waist. Once on land he pulled this until the light rope to which it was attached was in his hands. Then several villagers would help him pull the third line ashore—a heavy hawser. This would be made fast to a tree and the riverboat would swing into the muddy bank. If the long gangplank that was swung out did not quite reach dry land, the porters and passengers waded the last few yards to and from the shore.

On the Irrawaddy we tied up for the night but not so on the Congo. We sat on deck late, fascinated by the changing scene. As the sun sank, its golden rays appeared amber-colored in the reflection from the dirty brown water.

As we glided past small settlements on the riverbank, we would hear the Africans calling to us but they were undiscernible in the deep shadows cast by the full moon. Occasionally we saw the light of a small cooking fire. Once about midnight we seemed to be sailing right into the jungle. At the last minute we saw in the searchlight beam a narrow channel between the shore and a large island. We could almost touch the dense foliage on either side.

The second afternoon one of our barges ran on a sandbar and the lines holding the *Wagenia* snapped. The resulting confusion delayed us several hours and we barely made our plane from Coquilhatville to Léopoldville, now called Kinshasa.

We found the latter a surprisingly modern city with many tall white buildings. The new university was not yet completed and the first class had not yet been graduated.

Mary left us to fly to Kano, Nigeria. Charlie and I had a day to wait before getting a plane back to the Air Force and business, respectively. We decided we would like to try to get to Brazzaville, in the French Congo, just across the river. There had been a serious riot two nights before and we wanted to see what was going on.

The trouble had not been between whites and blacks, but between blacks and blacks. In a recent local election the vote had been split between two tribes twenty-five to twenty-four. In the first meeting of the new council one member of the majority cast his vote with the twenty-four of the minority. He reputedly had been bribed.

Out came the machetes and the butchering began. It went on most of the night. Not only were dozens killed, but scores were horribly mutilated.

We finally wangled a pass through American Express. Their representative came with us in a small ferry across the river. We were surprised when he said "Good-bye" and returned with the boat.

Charlie and I finally got a taxi and told the driver we

wanted to see where the trouble had taken place thirty-six hours before.

We found the native section enclosed by a fence. We were allowed to enter only after we and our car had been searched for weapons. There was really very little to see—just a typical African city slum area with no signs of violence. We drove through the native section. On the other side we saw a hundred or more French paratroopers who had just been flown in to keep order.

After Léopoldville, Brazzaville seemed to us a really "hick" town. It was much smaller than we expected. Most of the buildings were shoddy and needed paint. There was grass growing in many of the streets. On the outskirts of town there was a long, low, modern, attractive hotel. We went there for drinks and lunch. At the bar we met half a dozen reporters and broadcasters who had just flown in.

We flew out over the jungle where a few years later Dag Hammarskjöld was to die in an airplane crash under mysterious circumstances. With him, for all practical purposes, died the United Nations.

BOOLA BOOLA

5

A White Rolls-Royce
in Darkest Africa

IN 1963, four years after our Congo River trip, Mary and I
"explored" another African river. I use the word "explored"
advisedly since the river's name is as little known as the river
itself. We had not only read about but seen the Nile, Zam-
bezi and Congo. We had never heard of the Gambia River.
In the five years since, we have yet to meet anyone who is
aware of its existence

Early in February, Junkie Fleischmann asked us to join
him and Dorette, and Ralph and DeWitt Hanes at Dakar,
Senegal, and cruise north to the Mediterranean on his yacht,
Camargo IV.

I bought a map of West Africa to see what ports we might
stop at on the way. A quick glance showed there were
almost none. To the south we saw many with fascinating
names and for the first time, the Gambia River.

Mary had hardly said, "Wouldn't it be great to cruise up the Gambia" when the phone rang. It was Junkie calling from Cincinnati. "I've been looking at maps and I think it would be more interesting to go south and particularly up the Gambia River." Mary couldn't have done better if she had rubbed a lamp.

Gambia is a splinter driven into the heart of Senegal. It follows the river for three hundred miles eastward into the heart of Africa. The country varies in width from seven to fifteen miles, half on each side of the river. The European language spoken there is English in contrast to French-speaking Senegal, which surrounds Gambia.

We spent five unscheduled days in Dakar awaiting the arrival of *Camargo IV*, which had been delayed by severe storms in the Mediterranean and in the Atlantic south of Gibraltar.

We were thankful for this unexpected change in plans. Dakar is a surprisingly modern city with an outstanding colorful market, but what fascinated us most were the people. Many of the men were handsome and the women beautiful. No two women dress alike. A rainbow would be ashamed to show itself in Dakar. The Senegalese are very black with fine features not usually found in Africa. They carry themselves erect with a self-assured dignity and pride that comes from within.

We visited the almost deserted island of Gore, from which were shipped more than half the slaves that went to America. It was as depressing to think that white men engaged in this shameful traffic as to remember that the potential slaves were captured and sold by their fellow Africans.

On Gore we saw the dungeons where the slaves were herded together before shipment. When one died he was pushed out a door into the sea. Many of his fellow prisoners must have envied him later.

When we finally left Dakar and passed close by Gore on our luxurious yacht, I thought of the poor wretches who had passed the same way battened below decks like animals. Not only was I depressed but somehow I had a feeling of guilt that their descendants were often being discriminated against today.

Though it was only ninety miles from Dakar to the mouth of the river, it was rough going. The 115-foot yacht wasn't doing too badly until her stabilizers broke down. Then we decided to sit or lie on the floor to prevent possible injury.

The stabilizers were repaired before we entered the mouth of the river. It was just as well, as there was little of the expected shelter there. At that point the river was twenty-seven miles wide.

It narrowed to seven miles at Bathurst, the capital, situated on an island. We tied up and caused a sensation. No one there had ever seen anything like *Camargo IV*. Few tourists ever get to Bathurst and those that do, do not arrive by yacht. Gambia is one of the few countries we have ever visited where it was impossible to buy postal cards.

The six of us went ashore immediately to see the city before sunset. There wasn't much to see.

An unpaved dirt road ran along the waterfront. On one side were a few small fishing vessels and on the other some dingy shops selling piece goods, or a limited assortment of canned goods, toilet articles, or kitchenware. We were escorted by a dozen fascinated teen-agers speaking pidgin English, and a few mongrel dogs.

They dropped us after a quarter of a mile when we left the "main street" behind and emerged into the country. We decided to continue on to the British Governor General's house and "sign the book" and then go a little farther and have a gin and tonic at the one hotel. It wasn't hard to find the way as there was only one road.

A car stopped and offered us a lift. The occupants were

the British Governor General and his wife, and Sir John and Lady Paul. After introductions, they asked us to come for cocktails in three-quarters of an hour.

The Pauls served cocktails in the garden of their lovely house. There were eight acres of tropical trees and flowers and a large area devoted to vegetables and English flowers.

The next morning we started up the Gambia River. It cannot be called a forgotten river because it has never been known. A month earlier, none of us had ever heard of it. Besides being one of the big rivers of the world, it is certainly one of the loveliest. It rises in Central Africa and flows hundreds of miles to the sea. The Portuguese, who discovered it, and other early explorers thought it was one of the mouths of the Nile.

It has changed little since their day. Because the river rises thirty feet during the rainy season, no one lives along the low banks. There are only two permanent towns east of Bathurst and each of these has less than a thousand inhabitants. Both are built on high bluffs, Georgetown 125 miles up the river, and Basse twice that distance. There were six whites in each town.

There are about a dozen temporary villages of a few huts each where the ground nuts (peanuts) are loaded during the dry season. Otherwise the river has not changed in the nearly five hundred years since its discovery.

As our native pilot guided us slowly up the river, we realized that we were seeing what the Portuguese explorers saw. Nothing had changed. Perhaps the mangrove trees were taller. They were more than sixty feet high. A hundred miles up the river they gave way to palm trees and jungle growth.

It was so still we could hear the birds singing and calling to each other when the channel swung close to shore. Eagles became as commonplace as waterfalls in Norway. We could often spot them half a mile away without binoculars. Usually they perched on the very tops of dead or leafless trees. Their white, regally held heads stood out against the green of the jungle foliage.

We wondered why we saw so few fishermen out in their dugout canoes. We would often go hours at a time without seeing any human life. When we visited our first little village we discovered the reason.

Several times we had to wait for the rising tide in shallow parts of the river. Its action extends more than a hundred miles inland.

On one of these occasions, the starboard launch was lowered and we chugged several miles up a small tributary stream. The jungle met overhead. Twice as we rounded a bend sleepy-eyed crocodiles slid down the muddy bank into the water. Many of the trees were festooned with the nests of weaver birds that hang down like Christmas tree decorations. A few baboons scampered in the underbrush.

Suddenly we came upon a small village in a little clearing in the jungle. Many of the women, naked to the waist, rushed into their huts to put on their finest clothing.

One little boy was anxious to have his old grandmother meet the girls. When they approached her house she would not come out. She was confused as to their sex because all three were wearing pants. I suggested that the girls remove their blouses to reassure her but this did not prove necessary.

We men left them to explore the village. Suddenly we three Yale graduates were surprised to hear the chant, "Boola, Boola." Around the corner came Mary at the head of a parade of about seventy-five children, leading them like a cheerleader. After that we taught the children in the villages to shout, "Boola, Boola" in unison. Any Harvard or Princeton men going up the river are in for a surprise. There probably will not be many of them. Father Brown told us at Basse that he had seen only one American there in fourteen years and he was from the Ford Foundation.

In the center of the village near the community well was

the Bantaba. This is a raised platform covered with straw mats usually shaded by a huge baobab tree. Since the men leave all the work to the women, they have nothing to do. They gather first thing in the morning on the Bantaba and spend the day dozing or gossiping. Since they are almost all illiterate and uneducated, we doubted if their conversation could have been very stimulating. They were probably reduced to talking about women—men's favorite subject the world over.

After seeing the Bantaba we understood the lack of fishermen. The men cultivate the ground nuts several times a year and help to gather them. Everything else is done by the women. They sow and harvest the millet, which is the staple part of their diet. They pound it in rough wooden vessels. Men like to have more than one wife to labor for them.

We visited several villages on our way up the river, all of them inland a mile or more. Once we hired a dilapidated Volkswagen bus at a peanut-loading dock for the trip over parallel ruts.

Each palm and bamboo hut has its own little compound enclosed in "Crinting"—neat fences woven of split bamboo.

The men dress in muumuus, long loose robes that look like old-fashioned night shirts. They are usually blue. Their long, pointed slippers are white or yellow. Junkie, Ralph, and I bought muumuus and also slippers. I bought a particularly beautiful pair of the latter in a small village market. A native who saw me carrying them wanted the slippers so badly that he offered me a goat in exchange. The deal fell through when Junkie said one of the rules of the *Camargo IV* was "no goats on board."

Most of the women working in the fields had babies strapped to their backs. The "pill" and the "loop" were unknown to them, I doubt if it would have made any difference if they had been available. Nature took care of the "population explosion." Half the children die before they reach their fifth birthday. We were told that 55 per cent of the natives have malaria regularly. There is little grief or ceremony at death. There are no cemeteries. The dead are buried in their own yard.

On the third day up the river we tied up at Georgetown, the third largest community in Gambia. We were met by the British commissioner, who had received word from Sir John Paul of our trip upriver. Two of the whites were away but we had the other four, the Gambian headmaster of the school and several other Gambians on board for dinner.

It must have been quite an event for them. Their only contact with even the rest of the Gambia was by shortwave radio and the monthly riverboat. The ruts to Bathurst were seldom used by either of the two jeeps in town.

Between Georgetown and Basse the river narrowed. Once as we skirted the bank at sunset, a whole tree came alive. We had not noticed the hundred or more baboons dozing in its branches. Many ran along the shore following us for a while.

The beautiful 115-foot white yacht flying the American flag was undoubtedly a surprise to the natives at Basse. We were equally surprised at the sight of a beautiful white Rolls-Royce waiting at the dock.

We learned later that it was the only automobile in town if you excepted a handful of jeeps. It was owned by the British commissioner, Gordon Edwards. He turned out to be the man on the dock who looked like a cross between George V and Falstaff. His enormous beard was white on the cheeks and black at the chin.

He took us at once to visit a school run by two Catholic nuns, looking cool in their starched immaculate white robes in spite of the intense heat. They offered us coffee or beer. It was so hot we all chose beer, expecting some local brew. Imagine our surprise when we were offered our choice of ice-cold Amstel, Heineken or Carlsberg in quart bottles—one for each of us.

We noticed that the half dozen flower beds in the little garden were bordered by the bottoms of beer bottles. The Mother said we were helping her well on her way to another flower bed. While we talked a little fawn peered in the doorway and then came in and lay down at the nun's feet. I thought of Bambi.

After our "coffee break" Mother Michael showed us about the school. There were half a dozen classrooms, each filled with girls of different ages, ranging from about six to fourteen. They were all neatly dressed in navy blue with white collars. Most Gambians are Moslems and the two nuns did nothing to try to convert them to Catholicism. They only wanted to educate them.

We were very much impressed with the school. After Christmas each year we send them a large box containing the cards we have received. Apparently they fascinate the children. We also send a small check annually to Mother Michael and she gives them a Christmas party, saying it is from their friends in the United States.

The most primitive tribe in Gambia is the Fula. Gordon Edwards took us to see one of their villages. We all crowded into his white Rolls-Royce. Even in such a good automobile it was rough going, though we were motoring on one of the half dozen miles of "road" around Basse. Following us in a jeep or Land-Rover were the Catholic priest who oversaw the school, and Peter Tremayne, the assistant commissioner. They, in turn, were followed by another Land-Rover. We guessed later that Gordon Edwards had the extra jeep ready because he feared what did happen.

At the first small bridge we had to abandon the Rolls because it was too low to the ground to cross. We piled into the two jeeps for the roughest ride I've ever had anywhere in the world. It wouldn't have been so bad if the drivers had not imagined themselves potential racing drivers—and they weren't even Italians.

It was so brutal sitting on the steel benches that we crouched hanging onto the beams supporting the canvas top.

The village was more primitive than any we had seen in Gambia. Several men were weaving narrow strips of cloth, manipulating the looms with their toes. For the first time we saw pottery jars made without a potter's wheel. They just revolved the clay in loose sand.

At dinner on board *Camargo IV* that evening, we had among the guests an extremely attractive young English nurse, Wendy Heller, who had just arrived at Basse after several years in Dahomey. Since there was no doctor nearer than Bathurst, 250 miles away, hers was quite a responsibility.

The other guests were Gordon Edwards, Peter Tremayne and Father Brown. Junkie had invited the two nuns but the rules of their order prevented their going out to dinner though they had inspected the yacht earlier in the day. Ice cream from the deep freeze was a special treat for some of the guests who had not had any in years.

That afternoon the Commissioner had dispatched a runner upriver to Fallatenda to tell the Seyfu (chief) of Wuli that we were coming by launch to call upon him the next day.

Our departure was delayed in the morning because of the failure of one of the outboards on the porch launch. It was never fixed and as a result, what should have been a two-hour trip took more than three hours. We didn't care. We hadn't come so far to hurry. We could do that at home.

One launch flew the American flag and the other, the Union Jack. The crewmen soon gave up their efforts to keep the two boats side by side for protocol reasons. Nobody else cared.

It was a fascinating trip. Only very small boats can navigate above Basse. Startled natives waved at us from the shore or scuttled into the jungle. Peter identified for us more than thirty different kinds of birds. Even I knew a hippo when I saw one. Some of the lizards were more than two feet long.

We were unprepared when we rounded a bend in the river and saw several hundred natives atop a bluff, waiting to welcome us. They were dressed in their finest and most colorful clothes, silhouetted against a cloudless blue sky.

We disembarked at a little dock at the foot of the bluff. The people above waved at us and shouted unintelligible greetings—obviously friendly.

As we struggled up the narrow path in the red clay we heard the sound of drums in the distance. When we reached the top of the bluff the noise of the tom-toms grew louder. A strange procession emerged from under the trees. At the head was the Seyfu of Wuli—a very tall man in a white robe and a red fez. He was carrying a very large and thin (apparently empty) briefcase, of which he obviously was very proud. He was flanked by two other tall men in white robes.

Behind the dignitaries were two men beating on native drums. They were followed by several hundred men, women and children in every conceivable dress. Some of the women's costumes were very beautiful and many wore large gold earrings. One young boy had acquired an old helmet of the type motorcyclists used to wear before they switched to crash helmets. He was enormously proud of it and wore it with the ear flaps down and dangling in spite of the heat.

We were introduced to the Seyfu and then, with the drummers leading the way, proceeded to a large square building open on three sides with a corrugated tin roof. Our party sat on a sort of stage while the Seyfu of Wuli faced us in the middle of the front row. His "throne" was a canvas deck chair with a carved headpiece.

The whole village crowded inside the meetinghouse or massed outside. The Seyfu welcomed us with a little speech from the throne, which was interpreted for us by Caramou, the Commissioner's "Man Friday." He said he had been Seyfu for nine years and his father for thirty-five years before him. Neither had ever had a "foreign visitor" before. (Ruling commissioners didn't count as "visitors" and they seldom went to Fallatenda.) He then presented Junkie with a rusty sword in a beautiful hand-woven scabbard.

Junkie thanked him and said we had come from far across the sea to bring him the best wishes of the American President and the American people. Before he finished there wasn't a dry eye in the house and I was reaching for my second handkerchief.

Meanwhile Gordon Edwards was taking down the proceedings on a transistorized tape recorder. When he played it back, he made Merlin look like a Little Leaguer. The faces were something to see.

A boy with a calabash stringed instrument sang an interminable song about some past war and then started to sing the praises of the Seyfu. It was like a king's troubadour of old. I realized that the troubadours had originated the singing commercial.

When the boy couldn't think of any more nice things to sing about the Seyfu, the meeting broke up and we all gathered outside to watch dancing. This was not organized. Men or women would get up when the spirit moved them, dance for a while, and then sit down. As the music became more and more frenzied, the dancing became more erotic.

We were told that the dancers would have danced better and with more energy and stamina if it were not for the fact that they had been observing Ramadan for nearly four weeks.

The Moslem Ramadan corresponds to our Lent, but is much more austere, even though it lasts thirty, not forty days. During that time a devout follower of the prophet fasts from sunrise to sunset. He not only does not eat anything, he takes no liquids of any kind, even though in many countries he may be parched by temperatures of one hundred degrees or more.

When we slipped and slid down the bank to our launches the people waved and called to us from above. As we rounded the bend that took us out of their sight, we could see the gaily colored throng and hear the hypnotic beat of the drums.

On our return trip down river, we anchored the last night off St. James Island, twenty miles above Bathurst. It was the first and only settlement in Gambia for several centuries. Though only two acres in area, it was considered the key to the river. Possession changed hands frequently between the Portuguese, French and English. It was like a game of musical chairs in which the winner had the seat pulled out from under him just after he had won.

There was no fresh water on the island, and the tidal river was salt at this point. The nearest shore and fresh water were more than a mile away. Once the winner had established himself on the island, one of the losers cut off his water supply. Then it was his turn to win and lose.

We went ashore as the sun was setting. Perhaps at high noon it would have seemed different. In the half-light of the sinking sun it was eerie and disquieting. Even the birds seemed subdued. The few rusting cannon and the crumbled fortifications were the only monuments to the men of three nations who had died there—not by a merciful gunshot but by thirst imposed by the lack of water.

They lived, fought and died to control a magnificent waterway that has never been properly understood, appreciated or utilized. This magnificent "thruway" from the heart of Africa to the sea is now blocked by petty African nationalism as effectively as it once was controlled by the garrisons on St. James Island.

We arrived at Bathurst Monday morning, about ten-thirty,

to find great confusion. Ramadan ends when two Moslems see the new moon. It was expected that this would happen Monday night, so the Governor General declared Tuesday a holiday.

Sunday night one Moslem in Bathurst claimed he had seen the new moon. Then it was announced over the radio that one had seen it in Senegal. This was followed by the announcement that seven had seen it in Mauretania. Some of them must have been climbing trees.

As a result of these announcements many Gambians concluded Ramadan was over and celebrated Monday. There were impromptu parades in the streets and the people were dressed in their best. It was an unscheduled double-header as they celebrated Tuesday also.

Junkie gave a reception on board *Camargo IV* Monday night for about forty people, one-third British, and two-thirds Gambian. When the last guests had left we accompanied Sir John and Lady Paul to their embassy residence for a delicious dinner of Gambian food served on priceless gold-bordered china. Concealed lights illuminated the beautiful garden.

On our way home we heard music and the sound of merriment. By this time everyone had agreed that Ramadan was over. We dismissed our car and went on foot so we could join the crowds and see what was going on.

At one place about fifty people were gathered in a small open space between two thatched huts. We wondered why they had formed a circle—at a distance—around what appeared to be a twelve-foot high haystack. It began to sway and twirl. From the terror in the faces of the onlookers we realized that we were about to witness a witch doctor going into his act. We never learned where the weird music came from. The haystack began to dance but we could see no feet, arms or face. The awe and dread of the natives were communicated to us. When the witch doctor charged the crowd, they ran screaming in panic.

That night I dreamed that the scarecrow of Oz had taken up Wheaties.

When we sailed away the next morning half the population of Bathurst was at the dock and along the shore to see us off. One Gambian even put out a small boat after us when our lines were cast off.

Both before and after going up the river, one of the sailors had been haggling with a peddler in Bathurst over a twelve-foot long snake skin without agreeing on the price. When he saw his customer sailing away, the peddler capitulated and followed him and the deal was consummated.

We went down the river without a pilot. Captain Watson said that the night before the pilot told him how much he had enjoyed the trip on *Camargo IV* since it was his first trip up the Gambia River!

Part Two

6

Landi Kotal Doesn't Tell Macy's

I TOOK a nine months' trip around the world in 1926 between graduation from Yale and starting work in the textile business. Since this was long before the days of airplanes and television, the world east of Suez was little known to most people and had a romantic and mysterious fascination that has long since been lost. I was writing Mary at the time though we were not engaged.

We were married in 1929 on a date that was to "Go down in infamy," December 7, the date of the Japanese sneak attack on Pearl Harbor.

Shortly after our marriage, Mary remarked that my trip had sounded wonderful and "Couldn't we go around the world together someday?"

"Yes, darling, to celebrate our twenty-fifth wedding anniversary," I promised.

When that day approached she wouldn't settle for Arpege. We waited until the middle of December so Charlie and Winston could accompany us for a few weeks during their Yale and Hotchkiss vacations. They turned back at Beirut, Lebanon, and Mary and I flew to Karachi, Pakistan. We were twelve hours late taking off and arrived after midnight.

We had been asked to stay with an old friend of ours, Mohammed Ali, who was then Prime Minister. Because of our delayed arrival he naturally could not meet us, but we were well taken care of by one of his aides, who showed us around the guest house that had been put at our disposal. When our baggage was brought to our room we decided there was some relationship between caste, duties and footwear.

The first bearer carried our two cameras and our coats. He wore dirty white sneakers.

The second bearer carried our two flight bags. He wore socks that were full of holes.

The third bearer struggled with our four big heavy bags. He was barefoot.

We found Karachi an interesting city. Since the India–Pakistan partition it had grown from three hundred thousand to more than a million. Traffic was heavy. Though there were many cars they were outnumbered by camel-drawn carts and bicycle rickshaws. It seemed incongruous to see barefoot women in saris or long robes and veils with slits for their eyes trudging past new office buildings or modern homes.

From Karachi we flew to Lahore. We found it one of the most fascinating and colorful cities in the world and feel sorry for cruise ship passengers who see only Karachi in Pakistan.

Lahore is a tourist's paradise. The street life is as varied and interesting as can be found anywhere in the world. The Pink Mosque is the one we like best of all we have seen. And then there are the Shalamar gardens.

Less well known than the Taj Mahal, they rival it in beauty. There are usually few visitors and when Mary and I went, we were almost alone—surrounded by the beauty of the pagodas and palaces reflected in the many pools. The water bubbled gently from one pool to another through canals bordered with flowers. The silence was broken only by the whispering water. Mary and I were entranced.

We wanted to return the next morning, but our schedule would not permit it. Instead, we motored from Lahore to Rawalpindi, arriving in time for lunch. We stayed at the hotel guest house which Mary described in a letter to the boys:

"The guest house was rather primitive but clean. What I mean by primitive is mostly the plumbing. Washbasin and tub drain onto the floor and out a back door. The toilet is a bucket and when you want 'service' there is always someone sitting outside, so you open the back door and things are done in the twinkle of an eye and everything is in order 'for the next time.' "

Just before dinner, we found our old friend, Sayed Masoom Shah waiting at the hotel. He had motored from Peshawar to meet us and escort us back there. We had known him in New York, where he represented his country at the United Nations. A chieftain of one of the tribes in the North-West Frontier Province, he studied law and became one of the leading citizens of Peshawar.

The next day we made several sight-seeing stops, including one at Taxla, where we could see the remnants of the different civilizations left behind by the conquerors: Roman, Greek and Mogul. We motored through a narrow gorge at the junction of the Kabul and Indus rivers, over a bridge and we were in the famous North-West Frontier Province. The people looked different and every man and boy had a rifle slung over his shoulder.

(This was Kipling country but I had lost some of my faith in him in 1927 when I went to Mandalay expecting

to see "China 'crost the bay." Instead I found that China
was two hundred miles to the east and the Bay of Bengal
two hundred miles to the west.)

We stopped in a small village, where rifles were being
made by hand, and then on to Peshawar, where we stayed
at Dean's Hotel as guests of Masoom Shah.

The next morning Masoom took us to the Aissakhwani
Bazaar—the Bazaar of Storytellers, for in the old days it used
to be frequented by storytellers. People would gather around
to hear them tell tales of romance, travel or tribal feuds.
Here Kipling got ideas for many of his short stories.

The bazaar was the most diversified, colorful, and fascinating we had seen up until that time, and we have visited
few to match it since. Perhaps it was the people who made
it so different. They had a rugged nobility, simplicity and
courtesy that was most engaging.

Many things in the bazaar appealed to us, but we soon
found we could not buy any of them. If we said we "liked"
or "wanted" anything, Masoom insisted upon buying it for
us. We soon ceased expressing our opinions.

The next day, Sunday, January 9, 1955, we made a trip
to the Khyber Pass. Since my earliest school days the very
mention of it had thrilled me. I had never dreamed that I
would ever see it.

We were accompanied by Masoom and another friend,
Abdullah Serai. At first the ground was flat but soon we
were among hills that became higher and steeper as we
approached the pass itself. Ancient buses rolled by crowded
with humanity. Usually, there would be several men and
boys sitting on the spare tire at the rear—each with a rifle
slung over his shoulder. The approach of each dilapidated
vehicle was heralded by a cloud of dust several miles away.
There were many camels, some alone with a lone armed
rider on its back. Others were in long caravans, each animal
heavily laden and the men walking.

Most of the houses were of mud enclosed in a mud wall with small openings for rifle barrels. Without exception, every house had a watchtower with apertures facing in four directions. Sometimes a number of houses were gathered together in a fortified compound.

The road was primitive and wound back and forth through the hills as it gradually ascended. Since the camels needed only a narrow trail there were many short cuts for them. At the junction of the road and a caravan trail there were signs—a picture of a camel pointing one way, and a picture of a car pointing the other.

All the great conquerors since Alexander the Great and Genghis Khan had led their hordes through this pass. Here the Afghans had turned back the British time and again. There were many monuments to ancient battles.

About a hundred yards short of the border between Pakistan and Afghanistan we came upon a group of about a dozen men roasting a baby lamb on a spit over an open fire. It turned out that it was for us!

Several months before we had received a telephone call in our apartment from a stranger, Fidah Khan. He explained that he was from Peshawar and had been sent to represent his country at the UN. He had a letter of introduction to us.

We learned that though he had been in New York three days, he had not been out of his hotel room. He was scared to death, as he had never left Peshawar before.

Mary and I were just going out to a dinner party, but Charlie broke a date and spent the evening with Fidah Khan. We subsequently had him to our apartment a number of times and introduced him to Americans of his own age.

Word of our kindness to him traveled back to the Khyber Pass and these were his relatives expressing their gratitude to us.

Bread was baking in the coals, there were rice and a number of dishes we could not identify. Mary whispered,

"To hell with dysentery." We ate as much as we could but it was only eleven o'clock in the morning.

I was given a dagger and Mary, a pair of slippers woven by members of the tribe. They asked us back to their village but as it was a rugged two-mile walk each way, we had to refuse. Our U.S. representatives in Peshawar said they had never heard of a foreigner being asked to one of the tribal villages.

On our return trip about half a mile from the border we turned off the road for a few hundred yards. There, behind a low hill, was Landi Kotal.

Here the caravans rested before or after undertaking the arduous fifteen-day trip between there and Kabul. Many camels were lying down next to their heavy loads. Others were being piled higher and higher with boxes and bundles. We kept watching for that last straw.

In the hour we spent at Landi Kotal two weary caravans trudged in—one with about a dozen camels, and the other with about twenty.

There were a number of stalls scattered about with the most amazing assortment of merchandise we had ever seen in one place. Macy's may tell Gimbel's but Landi Kotal doesn't tell Macy's.

We recognized American cigarettes, French perfumes, jade from China, ivory carvings from Africa, saris from India, etc. Some things we could not identify. Everything had been smuggled in or was about to be smuggled out.

We were intrigued by one dilapidated six-seated bus that was just setting out for Peshawar. The first two seats were marked first class, the second two—second class, and the last two—third class. When we asked why the difference, we were told that it was because the dust clouds were thicker toward the rear of the vehicle.

From Pakistan we planned to fly to Kabul, Afghanistan, returning from Peshawar to Karachi to do so. When changes in airline schedules made this impossible we decided to forego Afghanistan and go directly to India. The only alternative was a rough all-night motor trip over one of the worst and most dangerous roads in the world through the Khyber Pass.

When our Embassy in Kabul learned of our change in plans there apparently was consternation there. Unknown to us, the Afghan ladies had planned a dinner in Mary's honor as the U.S. Representative on the United Nations Commission on Human Rights. This would be the first time in the history of their country that Afghan ladies would meet and entertain a "foreign" lady.

Our Embassy officials thought this contact with the wives of the leaders of Afghanistan so important that it was arranged that the U.S. Air Attaché in Kabul would fly to Peshawar and pick us up.

We were therefore surprised when the assistant chief of protocol of Afghanistan arrived with a car to take us to Kabul if we could not fly because of weather conditions. We demurred at the thought but he was so insistent that we nicknamed him "Frank Buck" ("Bring them back alive").

He was at the airport the next morning to be sure we got off all right.

7

Sewers Are Not
for Party Dresses

"THIRTY-SEVEN, thirty-eight, thirty-nine. There are thirty-nine camels in that caravan," said Mary. I wasn't sure the count was absolutely correct. Mary is prone to what Charlie, Winston and I refer to as "Pillsbury exaggeration."

Anyway, there were a lot of camels and we could see them easily. We were flying so low up the Khyber Pass that its peaks towered over our wings on either side.

The camels were heavily loaded and swaying from side to side on the very edge of a precipice. I was glad I wasn't one of the half dozen riders, and equally happy that Mary and I weren't jouncing along the same road, on the long, hard motor trip from Peshawar to Kabul. Only a sudden clearing in the weather had made our flight possible.

No commercial planes are allowed to fly up or over the Khyber Pass and of course no military planes of other countries. Our attaché's plane was the lone exception in 1955. Ours was, therefore, a unique experience.

We made the most of it. Colonel McKenzie, our pilot, pointed out objects of interest, but actually there were not many as such. There was only one village of any size between Peshawar and Kabul. It was little more than a cluster of mud huts. Its only connection with the outside world was the rutted track that we could see extending for miles across the flat and barren plateau between the Khyber Pass and the mountains encircling Kabul.

The slow-moving dust clouds below us hovered over camel caravans on their fifteen-day trip between Kabul and Peshawar. The faster-moving clouds were churned up by ancient model trucks. We could see them because they were just about able to outrun their own dust clouds. There weren't very many trucks. They were the only form of "modern" ground transportation in Afghanistan. There was not one mile of railroad in the country.

At the airport we were met by our ambassador, Angus Ward who had been a prisoner of the Red Chinese. Also our Afghan friend from the UN, Ambassador Pashwak, who was later to become President of the United Nations General Assembly.

He told us the government was going to put us up at their guest house but he thought we'd get more of the feel of the country if we stayed at the Kabul Hotel, the best in the country. Was he right!

Our hearts sank when we walked in. Seen from the street the hotel was the width of one doorway and one window. Inside the entrance a narrow stairway with a dirty, threadbare carpet led to the floor above. We went straight ahead down a narrow hallway into a small, fetid, overheated, smelly room. I presume it had a window but I have no recollection of seeing one. We quickly registered and were taken upstairs and shown to our rooms, which were in the new—not quite completed—wing, which could not be seen from the street. The hotel was bigger than it appeared to be.

Our kind Afghan hosts had provided us with a sitting room as well as bedroom and bath. The sitting room had no heat and was bone-chilling cold, and we only used it as a corridor to our bathroom. This was very large and very cold. There was a stack of firewood in the corner for stoking the hot water heater. Never having been a Boy Scout, the fault was probably mine, but I was never able to coax more than a few quarts of tepid water out of the tap, no matter how much wood I put on the fire.

The situation was better in the bedroom. The large iron stove in the corner was stoked intermittently day and night by little men with clean white turbans and dirty brown feet —all wonderfully friendly and good-natured. There was no way of keeping them out or of obtaining any privacy. Though the new wing had not yet been completed, the woodwork was so warped that the door could not be shut properly. Even if we had been able to close and lock it, it would not have made much difference. Instead of leaving room keys at the desk, each hotel guest was asked to put his under the rug in front of his door!—a custom that under-lined the decency and integrity of the people, rather than being a reflection on their intelligence.

Though the wing was new, the furnishings definitely were not. When, at our request, they brought in a second bed, Mary nearly fainted when she saw the mattress. She sprayed it with everything she had, including Lanvin's best toilet water. We thought maybe it had been the final resting-place of some dearly beloved camel.

After settling ourselves we went to call on the Foreign Minister, Prince Naim—a first cousin of the King. We found him a handsome, impressive, friendly man, well over six feet in height. He spoke of Afghanistan's friendship for the

United States, and his country's gratitude for long-term loans, technical assistance, and most of all, for the large dam we were building that would provide water to reclaim thousands of otherwise barren acres and provide much needed electric power.

Kabul, in 1955, was a very primitive city. Sanitation facilities were practically nonexistent. Deep open sewers called "Jeweys" ran down the sides of the streets. They were openly used by humans and animals alike—not only as sewers but for bathing and drinking.

There was little traffic in the dusty streets and what there was, was mostly animal drawn. Camels predominated, shuffling along with their sad eyes and pendulous lower lips.

We never saw a woman on the streets who was not heavily veiled. You sensed rather than saw the dark eyes peering at you through the mesh-covered slits. Their flowing burkas reached to their ankles. It was as though every day were Hallowe'en.

A woman whom I took to be pregnant from her silhouette, stumbled and fell just as she neared me. My instinct was to help her up, and then something stopped me—fortunately. Joe Donahue from our Embassy, who was with us at the time, said I would have been badly beaten by the crowds on the street if I had touched her.

I quickly gave up worrying about the effects of the fall on her pregnancy when I heard the crowing of the two roosters she was holding by the feet under her burka.

The Kabul River bisects the town, running between high walls to prevent floods. We were surprised to see dozens of oriental rugs hung over these walls, lending touches of color to an otherwise drab city. They were being beaten for hours at a time and unbelievable quantities of dirt were pounded out.

We learned why. After the hand-knotted rugs have been completed they are spread on the street for several weeks.

The traffic—camels, ox carts, occasional automobiles, etc.—wear the rugs smooth and pound down the knots. When the dirt has been beaten out they are ready for sale.

The bazaar fascinated us. The streets were very narrow and the open shops very small, usually nothing more than platforms raised several feet above the ground. The shopkeeper squatted among his wares. He, his family and his animals often lived underneath his "store."

Almost anything from any part of the world can be bought in the bazaar. Much of it is smuggled in on camel back over the hundreds of miles of unguarded and often undefined frontiers. Many of the shopkeepers were fierce-looking tribesmen. They probably did their own smuggling. Only Ali Baba was missing.

The backwardness of Afghanistan in 1955 was attributed by many to the Mullahs—the Moslem religious leaders. In 1928 they had rallied the tribesmen against the new liberal regime in Kabul, burned the schools and forced the abdication of King Abdulla and the reinstatement of purdah for women.

It was because of the strict enforcement of purdah that I was so delightfully surprised when I met, unveiled, a startlingly beautiful, dark-haired young girl with what are usually referred to as flashing eyes. I felt she should have been taming a wild horse.

Instead, she was working as secretary in the first maternity hospital in Afghanistan. I had a chance to talk with her and found she hated the veil and all that went with purdah.

Our first night in Kabul, we were invited to the Charlie Littles, friends of friends of ours, for dinner, at their house. They sent a car for us.

We stepped from our hotel into the dark, unlighted street. Mary was a dim silhouette ahead of me. Suddenly she disappeared. She had fallen into the Jewey which separated the sidewalks from the street. Fortunately it was the only dry one we ever saw in Kabul. I helped her out of the two foot deep sewer and into the car. We were relieved to find when we got to the Littles that she had only bruises and no open cut. I hated to think of the germs in that Jewey. The other guests welcomed her as the newest member of the "Jewey Club." All had stepped into one at least once—usually not dry.

The next night I went to Charlie Little's dinner for supervisors and technicians from the little-publicized dam the United States was building in the hinterland. Meanwhile, Mary was attending the dinner that was the prime reason for our being in Kabul.

There were about sixty ladies there of all ages—naturally no men. More than half wore Western dress, particularly the younger ones. The latter were rebellious and angry that they were subjected to purdah. The older ones were resigned.

After pomegranate cocktails more than a dozen courses were served and then Mary was presented with a full Afghanistan costume—beautiful pants, short skirt, shawl, blouse, shoes and silver jewelry (earrings, forehead piece, pin and arm and anklet bracelets).

The next day Mary was closely questioned by some of the Afghan men, who wanted to know what their friends' wives looked like.

The same day, Ambassador and Mrs. Ward gave a luncheon in our honor. It was particularly delicious as Mrs. Ward was French. We had a gay time and one of those present gave us such an amusing description of people in different countries that I wrote it down when we got home. Here it is.

South America
One South American—Siesta
Two South Americans—Fiesta
Three South Americans—Revolution

Scotland
One Scotsman—Perfect Host
Two Scotsmen—Dutch Treat
Three Scotsmen—Company Limited
United States
One American—Tremendous Plans
Two Americans—Tremendous Organization
Three Americans—Tremendous Confusion
Italy
One Italian—Conqueror
Two Italians—Opera
Three Italians—Retreat
Germany
One German—Philosopher
Two Germans—a Parade
Three Germans—Invasion
Russia
One Russian—One Suspecting
Two Russians—Two Suspecting
Three Russians—Concentration Camp

We returned to our hotel in time to receive His Highness's chief of protocol, who presented Mary with fifteen beautifully matched gray caracul skins as a gift from His Highness. We learned later that two sets of skins had been selected for then Vice President Nixon's wife to choose from. She chose the black set and Mary was given the gray one. Mary and Mrs. Nixon compared notes later.

Our original plans had called for our departure from Kabul for New Delhi by Air-India. When it appeared that Air-India would have to cancel its weekly flight, arrangements were made for Colonel McKenzie to fly us to Delhi. This was welcome news to a number of those at the Embassy who were overjoyed at the opportunity to go along on the round trip and spend a night outside of Kabul for a change.

At the last moment Air-India reinstated its flight, but by that time Mary had been scheduled to speak over "Radio

Kabul" and also to broadcast over the Voice of America. These appointments prevented our taking the Air-India flight. Needless to say, our friends at the Embassy were overjoyed.

As a matter of discretion, I've never asked Mary why she chose the times she did for her broadcasts. But I have my ideas.

8

A Vacuum Cleaner for
the Maharajah's Beard

WHEN Mary and I flew into *New* Delhi from Kabul in 1955
we went straight to *Old* Delhi to the Cecil Hotel, where I
had stayed nearly thirty years before. It was as I remembered it, old and worn and friendly with a charm that
aluminum, glass, chrome and air conditioning will never
achieve.

Old Delhi had not changed much. There were fewer
monkeys and not quite as many cattle on the sidewalks.
The latter are never molested because they are held sacred
by the Hindus. Who knows if that jowly steer on the doorsill
of the bank is not his own grandfather reincarnated. And
that knock-kneed cow might be one's mother-in-law.

New Delhi is the seventh Delhi. It had just been laid out
and construction started when I visited the site in 1927.
Now it had been completed. The pink sandstone government buildings are large and impressive and surrounded by

spacious lawns, trees and fountains. The Presidential Palace is huge and beautifully decorated with an outstanding garden. A series of large terraces descend in front of the Palace. Sculptured trees and an infinite variety of flowers are reflected in shallow pools. When one walks to the end of one terrace another one is revealed below, just as beautiful but different. At the far end there is a large oval sunken garden with a pool in the center. It is shaped like a sports stadium. The "spectators" are roses, snapdragons, petunias, pansies, etc. The "cheers" are the soft voices of birds.

The "Red Fort" in Delhi is misleadingly named. From the outside it looks like a gigantic fortress. Inside are some of the most beautiful and graceful palaces, temples and pavilions in the world. The interiors are softly lit by sunlight filtered through marble screens almost as delicate as lace. The lawns inside the Fort are beautifully kept as are the trees and flowers. There is none of the litter so characteristic of the parks in the United States.

Most tourists rushing from one Delhi sight-seeing "must" to another miss the beautiful gardens in the better residential neighborhoods. The Indians are like the English in their love of flowers. Whether this is a natural trait or one acquired during centuries of British rule is immaterial.

Instead of planting flowers directly in the ground, the majority are raised in gourd-shaped earthenware pots. These are frequently changed so that the blooms are always fresh. Cheap labor is probably the answer.

Since all my travel in India in 1927 had been by train at night, I had seen little of the countryside. This time Mary and I motored to Agra to see the Taj Mahal, stopping at Fatehpur Sikri on the way. Here a great courtyard is tiled like a Parcheesi board. Maharajahs seated in towers at each end played the game with girls as markers. For the first time we understood why Parcheesi is called "the royal game of India."

The graceful beauty and solemnity of the Taj Mahal

could never be exaggerated. It is hard to believe that mere
man ever created it. It has an ethereal quality I have never
seen in any other building.

The following morning Mary and I motored on to Jaipur.
Tourists who fly all over India miss a great deal. We loved
every minute of our two days by car. Besides the cows and
the monkeys, we saw many camels and a surprising number
of peacocks along the road. Many of the little bullock-drawn
carts were crowded with women in bright-colored saris.
Others, barefoot, walked with an easy grace. Whether their
magnificent carriage was due to the burdens on their heads
or their lack of high heels, I would not know.

It was a very dusty ride. Several years later in New York,
the Maharajah of Patiala, a Sikh, told Mary of the difficulty
he had with dust in his beard. Often after a long motor trip
he would not have time to wash and dry it before a luncheon
or dinner he was attending. I jokingly suggested to Mary
that we should give him a portable, battery-operated vacuum cleaner. Since she is not shy and was on friendly terms
with the Maharajah, she mentioned my suggestion to him.
He was enthusiastic about the idea so I agreed to get him
one.

Not trusting my memory, Mary phoned my secretary to
remind me. She was both amused and mystified when she
gave me the message:

"Don't forget the vacuum cleaner for the Maharajah's
beard."

Jaipur was even lovelier than I remembered it. Those
buildings that had not been built of pale pink sandstone
had been painted the same shade. Something new had been
added—or my recollection was faulty. From most of the second-floor balconies large squares of many-hued diaphanous
cloth reached nearly to the sidewalk. It was not being hung
out like laundry, but was held above and below by men who
were drying newly dyed cloth. To speed the process they

shook it slightly so that it undulated in the sun. I thought of a gentle breeze blowing over a field of daffodils, poppies and daisies.

We had met the Maharanee of Jaipur in New York and she asked us to stay at the palace as her guest, and to wire us when we got to New Delhi. We did so, but not having any word in return, we went straight to the Circuit House (Hotel) to be told that the Maharajah was awaiting us. His wire to us was not received until our return to New Delhi.

Our driver had told us that the Maharajah had moved out of his palace and built a small place in the country. We envisioned something like a large estate on Long Island or in Westchester. Instead, we drove up to a very large U-shaped white marble palace. The several doorways were guarded on either side by barefooted soldiers in neat, fancy uniforms carrying lances. We were led through a maze of rooms and seated on a bench facing an inner courtyard. We were left alone for about ten minutes and we began to wonder whether we were really expected. Finally a man in tennis clothes came and introduced himself to us as the A.D.C. (aide-de-camp). He led us past a beautiful sunken garden, across a hedge-enclosed croquet ground with a putting green surface, to a little garden and pool. Beyond the pool was a small attractive house which we took to be a guest house. We went through that and out upon the tennis courts. There were six beautiful grass ones in a row with a pavilion in the middle between the third and fourth courts.

The Maharanee and three or four others were having tea and two doubles matches were in progress. We were dirty and grimy from a long motor trip and had not been given a chance to freshen up. The fresh white tennis clothes made us feel even more unkempt.

We were shown to our rooms, the Spanish suite, consisting of a huge bedroom, large dressing room with day bed and two bathrooms. One servant was assigned to us. We roughed it at the Palace for nearly a week. It was a gay time with parties every night and polo matches every afternoon. Three Maharajahs who were playing in them were also staying in the Palace. One of them was the Maharajah of Cooch Behar, the brother of our hostess. Their mother was a lovely, older woman. Mary and she got along beautifully and she taught Mary how to chew betel nut, offering her spices from her silver box.

Her daughter, the Maharanee of Jaipur, is without question one of the great beauties of the world. Her pastel saris and fabulous jewels enhanced her raven-black hair and ivory skin. Her husband, Jai, was a charming and gracious host. We have been fortunate in seeing them in New York a number of times since our visit.

From Jaipur we flew to Benares by way of Delhi, where we again visited the Presidential Gardens. The contrast between this beauty and the depressing spectacle at Benares is shocking. Even though the rites there are carried on in the name of the Hindu god, one wonders if he can be pleased.

We took a small boat at dawn and cruised up and down the Ganges River along the ghats. At frequent intervals were wide series of steps. Instead of leading up into a soaring cathedral or synagogue they led down to the filthy Ganges. At the water's edge, men, women and children were dunking and bathing. They were crowded so close together that it was a little like performing one's ablutions in a flooded subway car. Some were quenching their thirst by lapping up the brown liquid specked with gray ashes from the burning ghats where faithful Hindus had just been cremated.

Though the rites at Benares were a depressing spectacle to us, they at least had the virtue of being prompted by faith. We could find no compensating factors in the sordidness of Calcutta with its million homeless sleeping on the sidewalks, its almost nonexistent sewage system and, worst of all, the complete indifference of the better-off Indians to these conditions.

When we flew out of India we had a feeling of relief. We had not been conscious of the depression that had slowly been creeping upon us. It was like leaving a late card game in a room that had become imperceptibly hotter and more smoke-filled and stepping out into a cool fall night under a star-filled sky.

9

Queens Should Learn to Swim

ON OUR way from Calcutta to Bangkok, Thailand, we stopped over for a few days in Rangoon. I wanted Mary to see the Schwe Dagon Pagoda and be exposed to the lovely, warmhearted, naive Burmese people. She enjoyed both.

The flight from Rangoon to Bangkok was a short one. Looking out the window, I could see the usual blue sky above and white clouds below. I contrasted this dull view with the sea voyage from Rangoon to Penang and the forty-eight hour train trip I had taken from there through the jungle to Bangkok in 1927. Then the city was known as the "Venice of the East" and the country as Siam. The change of the name to Thailand was as unfortunate as renaming Persia, Iran.

In Bangkok we were the guests of Prince Wan, the Foreign Minister, whom we had known in New York. We stayed in

Manangasilia House, which is more like a small palace than a home. Then Vice President Nixon and Mrs. Nixon had stayed there the year before.

Prince Wan was awaiting us in a private reception room at the airport when we arrived at 7:45 P.M. He told us that the Princess would join us at "our" house and that we would all have dinner together there.

We dined in the small upstairs dining room as the downstairs one was too large. It accommodated thirty people. Three times during the meal a little man with a DDT bomb crawled under the table and sprayed our ankles. The Princess apologized for the mosquitoes and warned us not to pick up any white winged flying insects except in a piece of paper. Apparently these insects could give you a bad skin infection. We never saw any. But we did see plenty of other kinds of small flying and crawling things. When I looked down into the sunken bathtub and saw all the bugs trying to destroy each other, I felt like a Roman emperor poised on the rim of the Colosseum.

Boys sprayed our rooms continually and we were given several insect bombs of our own. Apparently the insects were developing a resistance to DDT. Once when I sprayed a particularly large swarm of mosquitoes I thought I heard laughter.

Our beds were carefully screened and besides we soon learned that the mosquitoes seldom bit and they did not buzz at night.

The next morning as we drove around Bangkok I was disappointed at first. It had become a modern city. Most of the klongs, as the canals are called, had been filled in to make wide avenues and streets. It is as though Venetian canals were paved with concrete.

My disappointment evaporated when we caught our first glimpse of the Royal Palace. There is nothing in the world like it. The Taj Mahal is more beautiful, Notre Dame is more moving, Angkor Wat is more haunting, and Victoria Falls more majestic. But the Palace is more enchanting. The architect and Walt Disney should have wonderful aeons together in heaven.

The graceful curving roofs with their bright tiles, the delicate gold tracery around the windows, the fearsome demons and the sculptured trees combine to create an illusion of unreality. The Palace is just the largest and most beautiful of many, many fascinating temples and shrines. There are more things to photograph in Bangkok than in any other city in the world. And besides the "things" there are the people, not only on the streets but particularly on the remaining klongs and along the river.

We had a good opportunity to observe the latter as Prince Wan arranged a trip for us on the Chao Phraya River. Approaching the dock, we saw the preparations being made to welcome back a thousand Thai veterans of the United Nations forces in South Korea.

There were about twenty of us on the government yacht and lunch was served on board. We passed close to shore so that we could observe the river life. The small straw and bamboo huts were built on stilts over the water. Many had flowers growing over their roofs. Women were washing themselves, their children or their clothes, usually all three, in the dirty water. Sampans coasted by laden with all kinds of fresh vegetables and fruit. Occasionally we rocked in the wake of a small tug towing half a dozen barges piled high with rice. We saw several large rafts of teak logs underway but many more were tied along the shore, where the wood would be seasoned for a year before going to the lumber yards.

At one point we passed a shrine built at the spot where a queen had died. The boat on which she was traveling hit a rock and sank. She could not swim and drowned while her subjects looked on because she was too sacred to be touched by anyone but the king. Unfortunately he was not present.

On our last night, on the way to dinner, we stopped to have cocktails with our friend Jimmy Thompson. He had been in the OSS in the Far East during the war and had stayed on in Bangkok. He revived the old hand-woven Thai silk industry and spread its fame and products around the world. He probably did more than any person, Thai or foreigner, to stimulate interest in Thailand. His fabulous house is really seven beautiful Thai houses assembled into one amidst beautiful gardens and filled with priceless treasures he had collected in his many years in Thailand.

The Thais are a happy, carefree people. Perhaps their charm is due to the fact that they have never known foreign domination. The North Vietnamese are planning to overcome this oversight and have organized a Front to "liberate" them.

10

Cambodian Royalty
Has Strange Customs

FLYING into Cambodia from Thailand we had a wonderful aerial view of Angkor Wat, which we were to visit a few days later. Only in this way can one grasp the magnitude of this ancient ruin.

Our first day in Phnom Penh we visited the palace. The lovely, dignified, cultured, elderly lady who showed us around was very regal in her every attitude and gesture. This was understandable because both her father and mother were of the royal family—they were brother and sister!

Mary learned this from a member of the royal family at a large dinner our second night in Cambodia. She told me she never blinked an eye at the news but she did swallow hard. We had known that our unusually charming "guide" was the man's aunt but we were not aware of all the details of her ancestry.

The palace was like an illustration in a child's book of fairy stories in the days when children were fascinated by beauty and illusions and dreams—not murder and violence.

The Taj Mahal, the Red Fort and the palace in Bangkok are familiar to millions of people of all countries, even though they have never been more than a few hundred miles from home. Not so the Cambodian Royal Palace in Phnom Penh. I do not believe I have ever seen a picture of it except those that Mary and I took.

Actually, there are a number of beautiful, exotic buildings on the palace grounds. Their colorful roofs with their golden curlicues were breathtaking against a sky whose clear blue was accentuated by a few whipped-cream clouds.

As we entered and left each building "Auntie's" lady-in-waiting helped her take off and put on her shoes. The few workmen and others about the grounds groveled in front of her. She spoke to them in their language, not realizing we also had with us one who understood and later translated for us.

What she was saying was, "Do not prostrate yourself like that—particularly in front of foreigners. Don't you know we are a democratic country now?" This was early in 1955 when Cambodia, along with Laos and the two Vietnams, had recently become independent of the French.

Over the beautiful gold and white, intricately carved, jewel-encrusted throne was one of the nine-tiered, royal umbrellas that are always carried over his head whenever the King appears in public. The color changes with the time of the year and he always wears tight pants to match.

We were shown the crown jewels, but what interested us the most was a derby hat studded with enormous diamonds. The King of England had presented it to the King of Cambodia's grandfather so he would be properly dressed at Ascot.

The floor of the royal chapel is solid silver, beautifully

etched. Many of the offerings to the lovely Buddha had been made by members of the royal family.

Adjoining the palace enclosure on the Mekong River was a royal barge. We presumed it could move but it seemed to be permanently fixed in place at the end of two long booms affixed bow and stern with a gangplank amidships. The barge rose and fell with the water level like a float at a yacht club. Only here the difference between high and low water was thirty feet. It was not tidal but dependent upon the monsoon and dry seasons. The bank of the river in front of the palace was lined with huge stones built on a steep slope —like a medieval moat.

There is a hump in the bed of the Mekong River which prevents it flowing to the sea in the dry season. It then reverses itself and flows back into Phnom Penh.

When this occurs each year it is an occasion for a great ceremony and much jollification. The "King" gets tipped off ahead of time by the local equivalent of the Department of Water Supply. When the change of direction of the river is about to occur, he supposedly spends the night sleeping in the royal barge. According to the local gossip, he has upon several such occasions been observed sneaking back to one or more of his concubines for a few hours of rest and relaxation.

Anyway, he is always on the tethered royal barge when the change of current occurs. To demonstrate to the assembled thousands the miraculous reversal of the river's course, he throws a large branch on the water, ejaculating the Cambodian equivalent of "Eureka" or "*Mirabile Dictu.*"

King Canute should have had it so good!

One afternoon we went about forty miles into the country to visit a village that had been helped by the United Nations in the person of a Dr. Franz. Among other things, he had shown the people how to dig a well and they had struck water at forty feet. A large bag made of goatskins was dropped into the well on one end of a rope. The other was attached to a bicycle; when this was ridden down a steep bank, the water was brought to the surface and poured into a storage tank supplying the needs of the village. Before that the women had carried water in tin cans on their heads from a spring more than a mile away.

This village was formerly reached by two parallel ruts through the jungle. They twisted and turned for nearly ten miles from the main road though the village was less than two miles away as the crow flies. Since the villagers seldom had any reason to go to the road and thence to the city, this long way around made little difference to them. It was, however, a real hardship and delay for Dr. Franz on his almost daily trips.

To show their appreciation for all Dr. Franz was doing for them, the villagers decided to do something to shorten his trip. In the evenings, after work, they secretly built a direct road from their hamlet to the main artery, carefully leaving a few trees at each end to conceal their work.

When all was ready, these trees were cut down and the last few yards of road completed. The next day Dr. Franz was proudly shown the direct way home.

This was the road we took when we went to see the village, which we found very primitive. Many of the children were naked and the women were very shy. Most of them and the men as well had blackened their teeth because "only animals and bad spirits have white teeth." They said they were used to white men having white teeth.

Of those who did not have black teeth, many had red ones stained by chewing betel nut. Several of the more prosperous villagers had gone to a dentist to have him stencil spades, hearts, diamonds and clubs on their teeth! My surreptitious glances never revealed a full house—not even three of a kind.

We were warned not to pat the children on the head as this would implant evil spirits in them.

Not only the children but many of the adults felt Mary's clothes, shoes and particularly her stockings. The latter were always a source of wonder and astonishment to people who have never even worn shoes.

From Phnom Penh we flew to Siem Reap to visit Angkor Wat. Unfortunately, we had only one day there. It was an amazing experience. I use the word "experience" advisedly. It is not so much what you see at Angkor Wat as what you feel.

The whole complex of temples was buried and unknown for more than five hundred years and only excavated within the last century. Angkor Wat is by far the largest building of the ancient world. It covers five hundred acres and took fifty years to build in the twelfth century. Originally a Hindu temple, it was converted to a Buddhist one.

Angkor Wat is square and completely surrounded by a moat filled with water. High stone walls enclose a number of temples, galleries and libraries. We climbed up and down hundreds of very steep stone steps to view the carvings and sculptures.

There were only half a dozen other people in these monumental ruins. Everything was so quiet, you could "feel" the silence. We instinctively spoke in whispers.

There are hundreds of temples and palaces near Angkor Wat. About a mile away we visited Angkor Thom, a walled city that covered several thousand acres. Everything had been built on a colossal scale. The Terrace of the Elephants is nearly a quarter of a mile long.

We could feel the past and the jungle closing in on us. It was not only mysterious but a little terrifying. The trees were the tallest we had ever seen. We judged their height at 125 to 150 feet. Their roots had crumbled walls and split temples asunder. The trunks of the trees often began ten or fifteen feet above ground where a half dozen giant gnarled roots converged. I had the eerie impression that the land was not supporting the green dome above but that from on high giant arms with huge claws were clutching at mankind's past.

11

Butterflies on Wheels

FROM Angkor Wat we flew to Saigon, Vietnam, where we were guests of our Chargé d'Affaires Randolph Kidder and his wife Dottie. We had never met them before but we have seldom visited a more charming or relaxed couple. Evenings with them were a relief from our daytime activities.

The latter were interesting, unusual and depressing. We spent most of them in the refugee camps set up for the escapees from North Vietnam. I use the word "escapees" because that is what they were.

Though the Geneva agreements had been signed only three months before, the North Vietnamese had scrapped them within a month. Under the agreements any one in North Vietnam who wanted to go South had only to get to Haiphong, where he would be guaranteed free transportation. Any one in the South who wanted to go North was given the same guarantee. The choice had to be made by May 15, 1955, when the border between the two countries would be closed by a six-mile wide demilitarized zone.

The agreements were to be supervised and enforced by a commission of Canadians and Poles with an Indian as chairman. No serious effort was made to carry them out.

We talked to scores of refugees, many of them within less than twenty-four hours of their arrival. We learned that the North Vietnamese had devised many ways to impede the exodus from the North. Several women told us that when their family came to a river on their way to Haiphong the ferryman in the small sampan told them, "Women and children first" and never went back for the men. Some families went on, hoping their men would join them later, others turned back.

Would-be refugees who were lucky enough to get to Haiphong after weeks of walking were told to go back and bring their birth certificates before they could get their free pass South. (When I became eligible for Social Security it took me three months to prove I'd ever been born.)

When these harassing tactics slowed but did not stop the flight from the North, Ho Chi Minh threw a cordon of troops around Haiphong in violation of the Geneva agreements. This did not stop the exodus of people seeking to escape his rule.

We talked to those who did. They told us of their experiences. They had learned that the promised safe conduct through Haiphong was worthless. We wondered how they had reached the camps where we were talking to them.

Though their stories differed, the gist was the same. They bypassed Haiphong in favor of the coast. By that time the French and American navies had adapted to the new situation. There were few evacuees coming through Haiphong so they spread their ships at intervals three miles out off the coast of North Vietnam.

Hiding in the jungle would be a couple, a family or a whole village who had walked for miles to beat the May 15 deadline. One of their number would paddle out at night—find a rescue ship and arrange a rendezvous for the next night. Sometimes they would all make it in stolen sampans. But not always. Often the North Vietnamese would discover them and turn them back, with gunfire if necessary. Many drowned in their efforts to be free.

The optimists thought that perhaps as many as 400,000 North Vietnamese might choose to go South and plans were made to house and feed this number. They proved totally inadequate.

New camps had to be set up every few weeks. By early February, 650,000 refugees had fled the North and before the border was closed on May 15, 900,000 had "voted with their feet," and left the Communist North. Undoubtedly hundreds of thousands more would have left if the Reds had honored the Geneva agreements and not harassed and hindered the migration.

To reduce the exodus further Ho Chi Minh put on a tremendous propaganda campaign. Before the Geneva agreements it had been directed against the French and the Catholics. After that, against the United States.

We saw a good deal of the Minister for Refugees. He had lived for five years under the Communists. Unfortunately, he was never able to convince the Indians on the Control Commission what it meant to live under a Communist regime.

At first most of the refugees were peasants and fishermen, but as the May 5 deadline drew nearer, more and more small businessmen, white collar workers, and intellectuals trekked South. They had thought they could do business and live under a Communist regime. They had found out differently and realized the time for decision had arrived.

While Mary was speaking in French to the people in the

camps and having her words translated by priests or monks, I concentrated on the children. They had no toys so were fascinated when I made paper birds whose wings flapped when I pulled their tails. I spent more than two hours in a sweltering tent one afternoon turning out birds as fast as they brought me paper. There was little to be had and the children would search the camp for scraps. Once when I started to fold a piece of paper and turned it over, the children saw a picture of Christ on the other side. They insisted that this piece of paper not be used.

I was glad that the children climbed all over me. This reduced the area of my body open to the attacks of the voracious mosquitoes which filled the tent. I came down with malaria a few days later and always suspected that I got it that afternoon. It was worth it to bring a little happiness to so many who asked for so little.

On one occasion we had lunch in a refugee camp. It was tough going, particularly as every bite was black with flies.

One afternoon we were invited to call on the President, Diem. We were told that he was a shy man and would not "give, especially to a woman." He warmed up at once and told us what he was trying to do. He kept us an hour and a half and had tea served. We were very much impressed with him. We little guessed that in less than ten years the President of the United States would make a speech practically advocating his overthrow—but not his murder.

All of our time was not occupied by visiting refugees or making formal calls. One morning Dottie Kidder and a charming Vietnamese lady took us to see an old and typical Vietnamese house which contained a rare collection of china and jade. It was owned by an elderly gentleman who was delighted to show us his treasures and explain the old legends that went with the house: Why you had to go around a corner to go in (so your evil spirit wouldn't follow you); why you had to stoop to get through the doorway (reverence

and always remember the existence of a higher being), etc.
We spent more than two hours there and were fascinated.

That same day we learned of "Operation Brotherhood,"
sponsored by the Junior Chamber of Commerce of the
Philippines. They had decided that it was time Asians took
a part in helping fellow Asians. They raised money for
medicines and supplies and recruited volunteer doctors and
nurses.

We had tea with a team of about a dozen of them who
had flown in from Manila that morning. They would leave
the next morning for a Southern province that had been
under the control of the Viet Minh but had been ceded to
South Vietnam under the Geneva agreements. This, of
course, was a much smaller area than was turned over to the
Communists in the North. The big difference was that
nearly a million non-Communists fled from the North but
the Communists in the South were told to stay there. They
formed the pockets of resistance to the government which
have been at the bottom of the trouble in Vietnam ever
since.

Control of the province was supposed to pass to the government at midnight that night. No one could predict what
would happen but there was no doubt that the doctors and
nurses were faced with a dangerous situation.

The Junior Chamber of Commerce representative who
was in charge of the team told me, "We learned about helping others from the example set by you Americans." (A year
later Mary met the same team on an airplane. They were
returning to Vietnam after a Christmas holiday leave in
Manila.)

It is impossible to do justice to Vietnam without men-
tioning the women—or rather the girls. Whether they are
really the most attractive in the world or whether it is their
dress and hats which make them so fascinating, I wouldn't
know. The overall effect is what counts. They wear the

beautiful Au Dais. The underpart is like a fitted pair of pajamas with narrow trousers. It is usually white though sometimes the trousers are black. Over this they wear a gaily colored diaphanous garment with a high collar and tight bodice. It is slit at the waist into two panels that reach almost to the ground, front and back. They walk erect with good carriage and the panels float and swirl around them. Most wear large cone-shaped straw hats that nearly hide their jet black hair but only shade their large brown eyes. Most of them have waists about eighteen inches in circumference. Often they glide by noiselessly on bicycles, their bright "skirts" fluttering behind them. They give the appearance of giant butterflies.

One night we decided to do a little research on Vietnamese women. With a girl from our Embassy and a Canadian, we went to a real "joint" on the waterfront—where sailors go and pay ten cents a dance. The Madame joined us and we questioned her on what the girls were paid, how chosen, etc. As she talked, men came up and bought their dance tickets from her. One nice French sailor asked Mary to dance. She did so, but never got paid. Madame said, "He knew the difference and was trying to be polite and show you a good time."

The last night the Kidders gave a large dinner in our honor. Included among the guests was the French admiral who was in charge of evacuating whatever refugees could reach his ships. He was cooperating wholeheartedly; unlike many French officials who were sabotaging the migration.

12

Two Snakes and a White Mouse

FROM Saigon we flew to Taipei, Taiwan, with a few days in Manila and Hong Kong on the way. Our activities in these two cities were curtailed. I was alternating between shaking with chills and burning with fever. There was little doubt but that I had malaria though I did not consult a doctor. We did not want to have our itinerary interfered with.

Among those meeting us in Taipei at the foot of the plane's steps were two little four-year-old girls in costume. One presented Mary with a bunch of yellow roses and the other, me, with a bouquet of red ones. We had no trouble with formalities as we were the guests of President and Madame Chiang Kai-shek and were staying in their guest house.

The first night the Director of the Ministry of Foreign Affairs gave a dinner for us. There were twenty courses, but since it was Chinese food it was not as formidable as it sounds. We ate with chopsticks, to which we had long since become accustomed (I can manage anything with them except spaghetti).

The next day I took a "malaria break" but Mary went with Madame Chiang to see a camp for the Chinese prisoners captured in Korea who chose to go to Taiwan instead of returning home to their families. More than half of the prisoners made this decision. I doubt if they were all unhappily married.

We were in Taiwan at the start of the crisis over the offshore islands of Quemoy, Matsu and Taichen. The government decided to evacuate everyone from the latter as it was considered indefensible.

Mary visited the camp of the Taichen refugees two days after their evacuation to Taipei. They were a pitiful lot. Many had dug up the bones of their ancestors and brought them with them in urns and jars. Some had handfuls of dirt of their homeland in their pockets.

Though Madame Chiang Kai-shek was busy taking Mary around she was always very solicitous of my welfare. One morning when Mary was off with someone else, she came over to the guest house and sat and chatted with me while I had breakfast in bathrobe and slippers. She has the dignity and presence that used to be associated with the British royal family.

Our last night in Taipei President and Madame Chiang Kai-shek gave a dinner in our honor; out of deference to us the table was set with knives and forks instead of chopsticks. Mary sat next to the Generalissimo with an interpreter while I was next to Madame. After dinner I was assigned the interpreter and had a long conversation with the President. Talks with heads of state are seldom relaxing and interpreters do not add to the gaiety.

One incident made me believe that Chiang Kai-shek

understands more English than he admits. In discussing my travels he asked if I had seen the "snake farm" in Bangkok where serums were manufactured. I told him I had and that in one cage there were two huge snakes and one small white mouse. I said that the two snakes reminded me of Russia and Red China, and the mouse of Nehru. He laughed before the interpreter had an opportunity to translate. The next morning Madame told Mary he had enjoyed my story very much.

She took Mary to her studio just before we left and told her to select any painting she liked. Madame is an accomplished artist but her works are seldom seen. Mary made her choice and it was carefully wrapped for her before I saw it. I carried it gingerly for three days and two nights on our flight from Taipei to New York. What did it look like? I would have to wait until we arrived in New York to find out. She tried to describe the picture to me. She said it was "a beautiful graceful orchid in black and tones of gray."

She was right in so far as words can convey the beauty of a picture. Framed in the green mat which Madame had selected for her painting it hangs against the white wall in our dining room in Stamford. We have decorated our whole room around it.

Part Three

13

More Going Up Than Down

MARY went around the world again alone the following year, 1956. This time she traveled East to West. Though she financed her trip, it had the blessing of our State Department as a "goodwill" mission. She was responding to some of the many invitations to return that we had received the year before. Also there were invitations from her friends among the other delegates to the United Nations.

Our next plan to circle the earth together came about by chance.

If the S.S. *Dura* had not been set on fire by a bomb explosion in spring 1961 with the loss of 262 lives, we would never have known that there were ships with passenger accommodations running from Khorramshahr to Bombay. This was just one of those pieces of "incidental intelligence" that one reads in the Sunday papers on a rainy day in the

country. Mary was reading in bed upstairs in Stamford, and
I was reading another paper in the living room. By coinci-
dence, we picked up this same information at the same time.
We decided to look into the sailings of the British India
Line and then continue around the world.

Early in February in 1962, we left the luxurious International Hotel in Abadan, for Khorramshahr, half an hour
away. From there we took a launch down river for three
miles to the S.S. *Sirdhana* and were underway by 2:30 P.M.
The river was quite narrow at first, but was soon about half
a mile wide. It was the color of café au lait. There was not
much river life though we did pass a few dhows. They were
forty to fifty feet long, pointed at both ends, and with one
slanting sail amidship. Since they were made of teak, they
were unpainted. It was boats like these that we saw several
years later in Mombasa unloading Persian rugs.

As we slid down the river, the Iranian shore was to our
left and Iraq to our right. Soon the flat country on both
shores was covered as far as we could see with date palms.
We were told that we were passing through the largest date
plantation in the world—six million trees! There were occasional canals and ditches for irrigation. The few mud huts
we saw were protected from the river by a mud levee five
feet high.

We were glad to awaken the next morning and find everything normal. It was Saturday, February 3, 1962, the day that
so many astrologers and soothsayers had predicted was to be
Doomsday. On that date eight planets would be in line for
the first time in a thousand years.

Rough seas delayed our taking on a new pilot so we did
not land in Kuwait until 11:30 A.M. We were met by two
men from the Kuwait Foreign Office who whisked us ashore
without formalities though we had no visas.

We found Kuwait an amazingly modern and colorful city.
The tall buildings are gaily painted as a contrast to the
drabness of the surrounding desert. Thousands of trees have

been planted and watered by the slightly brackish water from the Sulaiba area wells. This is no longer needed for the people, as fresh water is distilled from the sea by large oil-burning plants, with electricity as a by-product. Kuwait is one of the richest oil-producing countries in the world. It is a socialized state as regards public education, health, roads, etc., but follows the free enterprise system in business.

Much as we enjoyed Kuwait, our whole trip in the Persian Gulf was really centered on the S.S. *Sirdhana*. She was only 8,200 tons but carried eighty passengers in combined first and second class, and 1,320 "unberthed" passengers. Our stateroom was originally a single one, but an upper berth had been added. There was a basin with running water and several communal showers nearby.

For the first two days we were the only "European" passengers. Occasionally a spook in white robes and bare feet would ghost down the corridors. We had the three-stool bar to ourselves and no one sat at the two tables for four.

We arrived in Bahrein five hours late, at one o'clock. The ship anchored about three miles offshore and we were not permitted to land. If we had had a visa for Bahrein, we would have not been allowed in Iran two weeks before because of friction between the two countries.

We gathered there was nothing to see in Bahrein, two islands linked by a causeway, so were glad to remain on board. The loading and unloading was an unbelievable sight. We watched for six hours, fascinated. The ship took on 750 "unberthed" passengers and disembarked about 150.

Most "unberthed" passengers were Indians or Pakistanis who had worked for several years in the oil fields and were going home "rich." Some had wives and children with them.

Below decks, Hindus and Moslems were herded together indiscriminately. Each one had about twelve square feet of space allotted. I figured that was six by two feet—the size of a coffin, which is what some of the passengers go ashore in.

There are frequent knifings below decks in fights between

Hindus and Moslems. Ships officers were never allowed to go below except in pairs. In spite of this precaution, one of the mates on the *Sirdhana* had been knifed in the back three months before and was still in the hospital.

The unberthed passengers came out in large flat-bottomed barges loaded with their belongings. At one time we had eleven barges tied up four and five abreast.

Their clothing was unbelievable. It was so dirty and bedraggled that any New York bowery bum put down in their midst would have been voted "best-dressed." Those that were not barefoot looked as though they had selected their footwear from the village dump.

The money that they had saved on clothing had been put into bicycles and transistor radios. About half the barefooted scarecrows had their radios turned on at full pitch. The Indians were tuned to one station and the Pakistanis to another; the result was not a lullaby.

Many of the women had wrapped themselves in their burkas and covered their faces. Some wore cheap, brightly colored saris. Nearly all were barefoot.

In addition to the overload of people, each barge was stacked with the personal belongings of the new arrivals, most of them in cheap tin trunks. The Moslems' trunks were decorated with paintings of mosques and the Hindus' with flowers.

Some had enormous bundles—large mats, rugs or blankets, with their possessions rolled inside. Many of these bundles were four or five feet in diameter and even longer.

A slanting stairway gangway was lowered to the nearest barge and then the fun began. Everyone on the barges grabbed everything he could carry and started jumping and clambering from one barge to another, making for the gangway.

Meanwhile those on the ship who were leaving, shouldered their possessions and started down the steps. Since there was no traffic control everything was soon in a "loose pandemonium" (a phrase a South American friend of ours used to describe conditions during a periodic revolutionary outbreak in his country).

Since there were 750 passengers boarding and only 150 leaving, those storming the ship soon asserted their right of way. If one of those disembarking was not too heavily burdened, he would climb over the gangway rail and work his way down the outside, leaping the last ten feet to a pitching and rolling barge.

When two six-foot bundles would clash head on, it was quite a sight. Once a large one was knocked off a man's shoulders. Luckily, it fell into one of the barges.

If things were difficult for the men, they were almost impossible for the women. Clad in their cumbersome black burkas, those descending crawled through the legs of the men coming up. The situation was further complicated for some of the women who wore long curving black beaks under their black veils. They were apparently fixed to their heads and foreheads in some way and extended to the ends of their noses about three inches in front of their faces.

As far as the men were concerned, the women might have been dogs crawling between their legs. If knighthood had ever been in flower in this part of the world, it had definitely withered.

This unequally matched ascending and descending went on for hours. Every little while another barge would arrive. From a distance, it looked as though it were piled high with a bundle of old rags.

In spite of all the confusion, most of the embarking and disembarking passengers remained patient and good-natured even though they would not give an inch.

One of the ship's officers told us about falcon hunting. On a previous trip a sheikh came aboard with twelve falcons, each with its own handler. A large tarpaulin was spread on deck and the birds were tethered on it. Each falcon was worth almost as much as an air-conditioned Cadillac.

On disembarking, the sheikh would start across the hard-packed desert in one of the latter. Land-Rovers would spread out on each side with the falcons. They would be released and fly miles until they sighted a bustard (not misspelled), which is like our wild turkey. The falcons would drive the bustards toward the sheikh's car. By pressing a button the window would be lowered, letting in the hot air for a moment but permitting a shot at the bustard. We never learned of the mortality rate among falcons.

Maybe the Soviets would do better if they gave the Arabs falcons instead of tanks.

We did not leave Bahrein until nine o'clock. While anchored in port the bar was closed out of respect for Moslems but drinks were served in the cabins. *Our* steward, who was also *the* steward, brought us two double martinis covered by a napkin. We hadn't enjoyed a drink as much since the repeal of prohibition.

When I think of prohibition I remember Henry Rowell's poem in his column in the *Yale Daily News*:

> Four and twenty Yankees
> Feeling very dry
> Took a trip to Canada
> To get a little rye.
>
> When the rye was opened
> They all began to sing
> "Who the hell is Coolidge
> God save the King."

The next morning we observed life aboard, concentrating on the unberthed passengers living on the decks. Most of the women were heavily veiled but some of them were smoking. Those with new sewing machines were stroking them affectionately. Even the most poorly dressed women, girls and female babies were wearing solid gold bracelets up to their elbows.

This is one way gold is brought from one country to another. It is a form of open smuggling. There is a good deal of secret smuggling of gold also, particularly through Dubai and Muscat.

Some slave trading was reputedly going on in Dubai and Muscat but not to the extent of that in Saudi Arabia.

Security precautions were very strict at all ports both on the dock and on the ship. There had been three bomb incidents on the line's ships in nine months. It was suspected that the bombs were being smuggled by followers of the Imam of Oman, who contested the Sultan of Muscat's rule over that state.

Fire arms were strictly forbidden but we saw a rifle being smuggled aboard. When the captain heard of it he had a fit, for as he said, "All you need is one rifle to start trouble." Not only was the situation tense between Indian and Pakistani, Hindu and Moslem, but also between Kuwait and Iraq, Iran and Bahrein—just to name a few of the quarreling nationalities swarming on the decks around and below us.

It was difficult for even first class passengers not disembarking to go ashore under normal conditions. A smallpox epidemic had brought about even stiffer restrictions.

Having survived "Doomsday," our next question was Dubai or not Dubai. We were doubtful of our chances of getting ashore there. But we had underestimated the courtesy, ingenuity and efficiency of the agent for the British India Line (who had been alerted about us) and the British oil man who came out to where the *Sirdhana* was anchored.

They had arranged for a native barge to take us into the town and up the little creek that bisected it. We were not permitted to land but we saw more than if we had walked around, as our time was short.

Though we were fascinated by the life of Dubai as we saw it, we were more interested in the primitive air conditioning. What appeared to be an oversized chimney on nearly every house was in reality a device to create a draft below. A tower of hard-baked mud ten feet high, it was concave on all four sides. As a result a breeze from any direction was trapped and funneled through a hole in the ceiling. If not exactly air conditioning, it was the equivalent of a fan.

We were late anchoring off Muscat the next afternoon, but there was more than enough light for us to read the names of ships painted or chiseled on the rocky cliffs extending out to sea from the small harbor. This custom has been going on for centuries and the rocks are covered with the faded names of ships of long ago. How the crews climbed to some places to paint them, we could not understand. We were glad to read *Sirdhana* and wondered why such an easily accessible space had been so conveniently left bare for so long.

Muscat is a town of about 3,500 squeezed in by hills of bare rock hundreds of feet high on three sides, and by a waterfront only a few hundred yards long on the other. Ships anchor outside and the barges go in through a narrow passage between the cliffs.

(Two years later we were reminded of Muscat when we anchored off Mutsamudu in the Comoro Islands on our way to Madagascar. No one was allowed ashore there as terrible storms frequently burst without warning and a ship has to put to sea at once. Though the two harbors are similar, Mutsamudu is even smaller and more primitive than Muscat. We counted only twenty-seven lights in Mutsamudu, probably kerosene. Ships stop there to unload supplies into pirogues only once every two months.)

At Muscat, there are two mud and stone forts on each side of the entrance. The one on the left is used as a jail. From the one on the right an ancient cannon is fired every night at three hours after sunset. Then the gates of the walled city are closed and no one is allowed in the streets without an oil lamp. Flashlights are not permitted because they can be turned off too easily. The streets are also patrolled.

We were told that there were thirty-eight prisoners in the fort used as a jail. This is the only place to incarcerate any offenders no matter how slight their offense. After dark, there were no lights showing and we concluded it must be a pretty dismal place.

A man convicted of murder is executed in a rather unusual way. The condemned is stood against a wall and a relative of the murdered man or woman gets three shots at him from a short distance.

We knew it was almost impossible to go ashore in Muscat so we pulled all the wires we could before leaving home. Sam Pryor of Pan American Airways had personally written to his friend the Sultan of Muscat in our behalf.

When a Mr. White from the steamship company came aboard with the customs officials and immediately sought us out, we concluded everything was arranged.

It was for Mary. For some reason never explained, only she was expected. There was no permit for me to go ashore.

Mr. White suggested that he send his barge in and get me a permit. I insisted that Mary go on this first trip and take both our cameras as it was five o'clock and the light was fading fast.

I was assured that the barge would be back in half an hour. Finally, at six-thirty, it returned with the following note from Mr. White.

"Dear Mr. Lord. I have been refused permission for you to come ashore. I will bring Mrs. Lord back with the captain at 7:45."

I decided the situation called for a drink. I asked the steward to bring me one double martini. Not understanding, he brought me the usual two, unaware that Mary was ashore.

They had just arrived when I heard a knock at the door.

I flipped off the light so as not to reveal the martinis if they were Muscat officials (I was beginning to feel more and more like James Bond).

It turned out to be Major Leslie Chauncey, the chief adviser to the Sultan, who had come out personally to get me! Only he could overrule the government officials.

It was dark when I got ashore but the major drove me around in his Land-Rover. Though it was only seven o'clock the streets were deserted and there were very few lights. It was quite mysterious and I felt as though I were living far in the past.

Then he took me to his house to meet his wife and have a drink. The other guests were Mary, the captain, and Mr. White.

The Chaunceys had lived in Muscat for eleven years. Theirs was a large two-storied Arab house with a patio in the center. The entrance was through two massive carved wooden doors from India.

Talking over the events of the day when we returned to our ship, Mary and I decided Major and Mrs. Chauncey were two of the nicest and most attractive people we had ever met.

Our next stop was at Gwadar across the gulf from Muscat. It had formerly belonged to the Sultan but was now part of Pakistan. An enclave in the latter country as Goa was in India, the Pakistanis could easily have taken it by force as the Indians seized Goa. Instead, they purchased it from the Sultan.

As in all the other ports except Kuwait, our ship had to anchor offshore. There were no motorized, only sailing, barges. Our stop there was a brief one, so we made up some of the time we had lost and arrived at Karachi only a little behind schedule. We were relieved to know that we would be able to catch our plane to New Delhi that day and make our connection to Khatmandu.

That is what we thought. We should have known better and counted on the inefficiency so commonplace east of Suez. Though there were few ships in the harbor, we waited more than three hours for a pilot. As a result, we missed our connections and were two days late getting to Nepal.

14

Orchid Houses Are
Not for Doomsday

OUR FLIGHT into Khatmandu, Nepal, was everything I thought it would be. It was a beautiful, clear, sunny day. For the last hour we flew about a thousand feet over a carpet of snow-white, fluffy clouds. To our left a few miles away, was the whole Himalayan Mountain range—the highest in the world. The rugged snow-encrusted peaks towered above us. It was hard to believe that men had ever climbed them. We could not see Mount Everest, but we got a wonderful view of Annapurna.

Occasionally we could see a rocky peak jutting through the clouds just below us. We began to wonder about getting down through the clouds.

About fifteen minutes out of Khatmandu, the clouds faded away and we began the long descent into the valley. It never snows there and the high but lower mountains around it were bare.

We skimmed only a few hundred feet over these mountains. They were terraced all the way to the summit. Occasionally we could see a path along the very top of a narrow ridge. It would be only a few feet wide with the ground falling away almost perpendicularly on each side.

Footpaths wound their way up from the valleys. There are almost no roads in Nepal, where the wheel is a relatively new discovery. The Nepalese carry almost everything on their backs with straps around their foreheads. Things not carried this way are suspended from both ends of a pole across their shoulders. The first automobiles were brought up in pieces on bearers' backs and reassembled there. All the furniture, etc., for the palaces was brought in the same way. A very poor road had recently been completed from Calcutta, a rough three-day trip to the border and one day over an even worse road from there to the capital. Almost everything is now brought in by plane—hence scarcities and high prices.

Khatmandu is very, very primitive. Automobiles that are too old even for Lima, Peru, end up in Nepal—but not many of them. It is hard to understand how they keep them operating since no spare parts are obtainable there or anywhere else in the world outside of museums.

The people in Nepal are miserably poor but the happiest, kindest people we had ever seen in all our travels. They are ragged, barefoot and dirty. Their faces are so wonderfully expressive that we wanted to take pictures of everyone we saw. Tibetan refugees were everywhere. They were taller and wore their hair longer than the Nepalese. If possible, they were even more patient and better-natured than the Nepalese.

We stayed with U.S. Ambassador Henry Stebbins and his British-born wife, Barbara. We had known them in the States and Mary had stayed with them in Khatmandu on a visit there a year before. They had been in Nepal for a number of years but had done such an outstanding job that our State Department and the Nepalese government both agreed they should extend their time there.

After luncheon with the Stebbinses, the first day, we walked through the streets for two hours, recognizing many of the places Winston had written about on his visit to Khatmandu four years earlier.

The fascinating bazaar surrounds the Machiendra Babal temple where both Buddhists and Hindus worship. Some women were sunning themselves on the various terraces while they waited for the laundry hung near them to dry. Others were busy searching their children's hair for lice.

Below them dogs and cows wandered among the fruits and vegetables displayed for sale on the filthy streets. The majority of the buildings are two stories high, with living quarters above and shops below. The latter are only about fifteen feet wide with doors that fold back like shutters. Almost without exception they were painted a dark red, almost the color of mahogany. Inside, the shopkeeper—often surrounded by his family—squatted amid his wares for hours at a time without making a sale or seeming to care.

I stopped and made a paper bird on the hood of an ancient automobile while children swarmed all over me. They were all talking at once and screaming with laughter. I thought it was just as well that I could not understand them as I gathered I was the butt of their jokes.

Our first night, the Stebbinses gave a large buffet supper and the next morning took us to see one of the Tibetan refugee camps. The ambassador had not been there before and was just as impressed and interested as we were.

Unlike most refugee camps we had visited in the Near East, India and Pakistan, these people were not left to rot. Nor were they being heartlessly used as political pawns the way the Arabs have used the Palestinian refugees since long before U Thant's Six Day War. (Nasser boasts that "the next time" the Egyptians will hold out for a whole week!)

The camp was run by the International Red Cross and manned mostly by the Swiss. Everyone was taught to do something. Women were combing wool by hand and spinning it into yarn. Then they wove it into cloth on primitive hand looms or made rugs. The men were learning the rudiments of carpentry—using hand saws and braces and bits for the first time.

The camp held two hundred and seventy refugees but was so full that they could not accept any more. We saw several dozen pitiful Tibetans begging to be let in; though unsuccessful, they still remained cheerful and smiling.

In all our travels, one thing Mary and I have learned is how much more kindness, friendliness and what we arrogantly call "the Christian Spirit" is shown by so-called primitive people than by those who consider themselves more civilized.

The Bil Baird troupe of puppeteers was touring Asia as one of the cultural teams sent out by our government. We saw one of their brilliant performances in the theater one night. Seven cents was charged for admission in order to keep the crowds manageable, but all six performances in Khatmandu were sold out.

Not content with their nightly paid performances, the Baird troupe traveled to the small towns in the daytime, putting on free shows in the village squares or any suitable place. We visited a hospital where they were putting on parts of their show in the wards. They were a sensation and many of the primitive patients seemed to think the puppets were alive.

There was no running water in the hospital, and mangy, filthy, mongrel dogs wandered through the corridors and between the beds. We were told conditions were much better than they used to be. Maybe that meant they had excluded the monkeys.

One day after lunch with the Stebbinses, we motored two

miles to the Golden Temple of Lord Suva at Pasupativah on the Bagmati River. This river is to the Nepalese what the Ganges at Benares is to the Indians. They all want to bathe in its muddy waters. Bodies are burned on ghats and the ashes thrown in the river. We saw smoke from one cremation a hundred yards downstream.

We then motored a short distance to the Bodnath Stupa, built two thousand years ago. Halfway to the top two huge eyes are painted on the temple. This was an important shrine to the Tibetans, who had been making pilgrimages there for centuries. With so many refugees from Tibet, the place was more crowded than ever. Many of them had settled around the stupa.

We went inside the dimly lit temple. Two rows of saffron-robed Buddhist priests—about ten to a row—faced each other in the center, chanting prayers aloud. We walked behind one row of priests and put an offering (as expected) in a box for that purpose. There were about a hundred silver cups filled with melted and often rancid butter. About half of them were lit like candles.

As in many other shrines, we were followed by a native orchestra chanting a singsong verse about Tenzing the Sherpa, who was one of the first two men to climb Mount Everest. He is the most famous Nepalese since Buddha. The song about him was the only one we ever heard.

One day we motored to Patan, the second largest city, a few miles away, and stopped in a large field where the Stebbinses said we would have privacy during our picnic lunch—provided by them.

They could not have been more wrong. We spread our cloth and opened up our delicious lunch. Before we had finished our first gimlet a small crowd had gathered and it kept growing.

In Nepal, as in all of Asia, cow dung is a valuable commodity. It is shaped into large flat cakes and plastered on house walls to dry. Then it is used for fuel for cooking.

All during our picnic, a little six-year-old girl stood right next to Mary. In her left hand held shoulder high, like a shot putter poised to throw, was a ball of fresh dung. Her little brother was towing behind him a piece of board on a cord like a sled. It, too, was piled high with fresh manure.

We were sitting under the only tree in the large field for shade. Halfway through our lunch an unseen bird in the tree made a direct hit on Mary's purse. The assembled throng roared with laughter. Then a little boy brought out his slingshot and shot a stone up into the tree. About twenty black and white birds took off and we were unmolested except for a cow that backed into me when I was not looking.

We subdivided our delicious chicken sandwiches into eight pieces and offered them to the children—after a tentative taste, most of them spit out the tiny morsels of American food.

When we had finished our far-from-private picnic, we motored into Patan where the Baird puppeteers were to put on a free show for the people. They had set up a stage in the village square, which was surrounded on three sides by temples.

It was a sight we will never forget—thousands of people in the most fascinating and varied of costumes, from rags to beautiful saris and many of the girls with bright ribbons or flowers in their hair. Most of the children were massed down front near the stage.

I took up my position about ten feet above the crowd on a temple platform and began taking pictures by the dozen. Half the time when I looked through my viewer I saw Mary's red bandana in the middle of the scene. She was everywhere, climbing temples, out on balconies, or just mingling with the crowds. She is an excellent photographer.

One night after their show, the Baird troupe was asked to

a buffet supper by Ambassador and Mrs. Stebbins. They were an interesting group. It was obvious from their conversation they were really enjoying the happiness they were giving to tens of thousands of people in countries where they ask for so little.

Mrs. Stebbins is an ardent and accomplished gardener, and they had a beautiful place. She was excited when we were there because she had just received some seed catalogues from her native England. They had recently built a small straw house for raising orchids. At that time the Nepalese were moving out of their houses into straw huts in preparation for the earthquakes that were supposed to accompany Doomsday, February 3, 1962. The Nepalese thought the Stebbins orchid house was for the same purpose. As a result, they had gained stature in the eyes of the Nepalese.

One day we motored to Bhadgaon, the third largest city, six miles away over a terrible road. It took us forty-five minutes. Winston had bettered that time on a bicycle.

The scenery made up for the roughness of the trip. Men, women and children were working in the fields. They break up clods of earth with primitive sledge hammers made of large rocks, fastened to poles. As usual we saw women washing clothes in dirty streams, pounding them on rocks and drying them in the sun.

There are a number of temples in Bhadgaon and we would have missed some of the best if it had not been for a nine-year-old boy who spoke fair English and was clean and neatly dressed. He acted as our guide and was warm and friendly.

There is a beautiful golden gate and some wonderful, well-preserved wood carving. The temples have more than the usual amount of pornography, which seems to go with the Hindu religion.

That evening we had cocktails alone with the third Prince

and a sari-clad American girl. The first Prince is the son of the King, the second is the King's brother, and the third is his cousin.

The same night the Stebbinses had the King and Queen and the second Prince and his wife for dinner—just the eight of us. We had met the King and Queen in New York and Mary and Charlie had taken them to Roosevelt Raceway one night.

Cocktails were served in the small upstairs sitting room and we returned there after dinner rather than to the more formal large room on the first floor. Perhaps it was the informality that made the evening so gay. There was good conversation and much laughter.

The King and Queen did not leave until 1:45 A.M. He drove her home in a European sports car. There was no indication of security precautions despite three recent assassination attempts on his life.

Our last day we flew to Pokhara, an hour and a half flight, to get a better view of the Himalayas, particularly Annapurna, of which we had seen only the top. At Pokhara, the mountains rise straight up from the plain and are therefore more impressive.

Unfortunately, there were many clouds and we caught only a brief glimpse of Annapurna. The trip was worth it, however.

Our first stop was at a small "airport" at Gurkha. It is from here that the famous Gurkha soldiers come. They are among the finest soldiers in the world—absolutely loyal and fearless. They are mercenaries that have been recruited mostly by the British in the past. They serve fifteen years and then return home "wealthy" with pensions. Their pay is the chief source of income in their part of the world.

The field at Gurkha is a cow pasture. When a plane is coming in they blow a siren and even the cows know enough to get off the field. It had only been open a few months and the people were trudging from miles around to see the planes. Some families walked all night. At first they brought hay to feed the planes.

There were no restrictions at the field and several hundred Nepalese of all ages swarmed around our plane—many of them stroking the wings.

The field at Pokhara is similar. There was one jeep that would take you to a lake and temple several miles away if you were lucky enough to get it. Unfortunately a Swiss medical mission needed the jeep for a ninety-mile trip into the interior.

We sat on the porch of the corrugated-tin government guest house and had another of the Stebbinses' delicious picnic lunches. We were pleased that this time we at least had a roof over our heads. We didn't have to waste half our lunch by giving it to Nepalese who didn't like it anyway.

We were glad we had saved some food when black clouds rolled in and it looked as though our return plane would not be able to land. If we had to spend the night in the hut at least we'd have a little something to eat. There was nothing to be had at the almost deserted airport.

We were relieved when the weather cleared and the ancient DC-3's arrival was signaled by a blast on the siren.

The next morning we regretfully said farewell to the Stebbinses. We have seen them several times since in the States and also at the coronation in Gangtok.

We have had a number of letters from the well-dressed boy who showed us around Bhadgaon. In most of them he asks for something like a watch, fountain pen, radio, or sweater, but even if we do not always send him what he requests he continues the largely one-way correspondence anyway. We did send him a cheap watch. Unfortunately (if he is to be believed) a school bus in which he was riding was in a bad accident of which he was the only survivor. As luck would have it, his watch was broken. "Please send another one."

Here is a typical letter.

Dated June 5, 1967

Honourable Mrs. Oswald B. Lord
    May it please your Grace.
Dear Madam
    I received your kind letter on May. I could not write you for a
long day because I am suffering from disease. Now a days I am
in the hospital. So please pardon me. The doctor told that my
health was in bad condition. He advised me to live in Kashmir
for one month. Kashmir lies in the north part of India. There
the climate is very good. By which I will be cure soon. But know
well that I am a poor boy so how can I go live there for one
month. I trust God will save me. But so long as I am alive I
never forget your kindness. You had written in the letter that
you would send me books from time to time. I request you to
send me the *National Geographic Magazine* also from time to
time. I must see many kind books for having good knowledge.
But we have no public library in our country so I implore you
to send books and magazines from time to time. I hope you will
be please to send it. There is none except you who love me as
her own issue. I hope there you will be well. Hoping to hear
from you soon.
    Praying to God to give you happy long life and health for ever.
    Yours greatful.

    The most pathetic and disturbing letter Mary ever got
was received just after her appointment to the Commission
on Human Rights.
    It was addressed to "Mrs. Oswald B. Lord, successor to
Mrs. Eleanor Roosevelt, New York City."

Dear Mrs. Lord
    I am waiting for you and Abraham Lincoln to come and save
me. They say I am crazy but there is nothing wrong with me
except my feet hurt.

15

Nothing Missed but Two Martinis

FROM NEPAL we flew to New Delhi, where we spent several days being entertained by our warmhearted Indian friends. We had seen all the "sights" on our previous visits but we did revisit the marvelous Red Fort and Presidential Gardens. We did little shopping as Indian merchants are so aggressive as to make it unpleasant.

For the first time we visited the southern part of India, picking up a car and driver in Bangalore and motoring south and then east. This was the most prosperous part of India we had ever seen. The people were better dressed and seemed to have more ambition. This was and is the most communistic part of India-Kerala.

The government had taken over the Maharajah's palaces and was operating them as hotels as well as other hotels formerly managed by the English. We did not mind the spotted tablecloths and dirty linen so much as the wildlife.

I am not referring to the ever-present cockroaches and lizards —no one can really do anything about them. In one hotel we got rid of a bat in our bedroom by chasing him into the bathroom and shutting the door.

In the same hotel we learned that the crash we heard next door in the night was the bed lamp being knocked over by a rat.

One morning I was having breakfast alone in a large, high-ceilinged, unscreened dining room. Ravens were flying in and out picking up crumbs. One particularly friendly one sat at the end of my table and ate the crumbs that I tossed to it. I would have thought that he had read my mind if he had croaked, "Nevermore."

We enjoyed our motor trip even though Mary's long-time ulcer was causing her great pain. She is so stoical and brave it was hard to know how much she was suffering. By the time we got to Madras she was writhing in pain and we decided to call off the rest of the trip. For the second time Mary left Madras for an operation. This time in New York.

On her trip alone in 1956, while in India, a long-time cyst on the back of her neck began acting up. By the time she was ready to leave Madras, an American friend insisted that she call a doctor. He said that the cyst was infected and that Mary must see a doctor in Colombo when she arrived in Ceylon the next day.

After she had settled herself in Ambassador Philip Crowe's guest room the doctor was called. Mary wrote:

"At 7:00 P.M., my first night in Colombo, the doctor came (a Ceylonese graduate of London and excellent). He took one look and said, 'This must come out at once.'

"He said he would operate either first thing in the morning or that night if he could get the operating room, an anesthetist, etc. As I had important dates with both the Governor General and the Prime Minister the next day— plus a luncheon in my honor and the Ambassador's dinner —I said, 'Let's do it tonight.'

"At seven-thirty the decision was made and at eight-thirty I was at the nursing home.

"Then started my experiences, which both at the time and now amuse me so I'll always remember that night! First there was no room in the main building, so when I arrived the sister said, 'Oh, Mrs. Lord—you are the patient for maternity.' I thought—wait until Os hears this news.

"I soon found out that due to lack of room I was in the maternity cottage—two city blocks away from the hospital proper. The only nurse on duty 'prepared me' and put on the usual hospital robe, open down the back, and the usual operating socks. She gave me a hypodermic to make me drowsy before ether. Then she announced, 'I must run to the operating room to scrub up and be ready to help the doctor as I am the only nurse available.'

"Just as I was really drowsy, a dear little dark man, barefoot in his white bangha, came into my room. And just then the monsoon rain, accompanied by lightning and thunder, burst in a blinding and furious downpour. 'Lady you come now—doctor and nurse ready—doctor waiting in operating room.'

"I gulped (semiconscious), looked outdoors at the rain and wondered how I could walk across a muddy field with my behind exposed and pick my way in my hospital socks. 'Raining, how do I go?' 'Yes, lady, much rain. Maybe I find umbrella.' (There were no other patients in the cottage—only an old ayah by a stove.)

"I groggily put on high-heeled patent leather shoes over my socks, a towel around my head (to keep my new wave in) and didn't care about my exposed behind, as I knew the boy would be walking ahead with the umbrella.

"We started out—I leaning on his shoulder as I was half asleep and he with his bare feet sloshing in the mud, holding the umbrella too high over my head. We arrived safely and I found out later that the sudden storm had caught the doctor and nurse by surprise. As they were all scrubbed and everything sterilized they *had* to count on my getting myself there.

"I climbed up on the table in the open-sided operating room. A few new recruits had gathered, including an excellent anesthetist. Two more hypodermics and I was out like a light, and then, I gather, ether after that.

"The last thing I heard as the lightning and thunder flashed and rumbled was the doctor grumbling 'nice night for an operation.'

"The actual operation only lasted ten minutes and I came to with no after effects of nausea, etc. The cyst, believe it or not, had grown almost to the size of a baseball (say a large golf ball) and was thoroughly infected. I did lose quite a lot of blood but had no after effects.

"This time I did *not* have to walk. On the return trip six little men hoisted a stretcher on their heads, while a seventh tried to keep me covered with an umbrella and off we went to the maternity cottage. Sort of funny riding on a stretcher at that height. I was given an injection and went off in a delicious sleep.

"However, just like all hospitals, at six-thirty when I was sleeping soundly a nurse's aide shook me. 'I came to bathe you.' I announced that I'd bathe myself. She said, 'No— you'll be wobbly.' We compromised and instead of taking a bath, I just washed at the basin. I then waited an hour for breakfast!

"I ate a huge one, as I had no dinner the night before. At eight-thirty I asked them to please send for the Embassy car. They were horrified and the matron came over and said a few days in bed were 'usual.' I said I felt fine—I had a full schedule—and asked her to check with the doctor. He said if I did not feel weak I could leave.

"So at nine I was back at the Embassy and Phil Crowe said, 'All you have missed so far on your trip are two martinis and a dinner.'"

Part Four

16

Turtles Are Patriotic

"YOU WILL have luncheon at the coronation reception at the Bagdogra airport. A car will take you from there to Gangtok. There you have been assigned guest room Number One in Royal Guest House Number One."

It was the Sikkimese representative in Calcutta who gave us these instructions upon our arrival on a through flight from New York. Mary and I had planned to go around the world from East to West in the early spring of 1965. Charlie and his wife Gay would accompany us through Japan. Then they would continue on by way of Hong Kong, Thailand and India while Mary and I would travel through Siberia, Outer Mongolia, and Russia.

When we were invited to attend the coronation of the Maharajah and Maharanee of Sikkim as the Choygal (King) and Gyalino (Queen) as their guests, we thought the occasion one too unusual to be missed. We changed our plans and flew eastward from New York direct to Calcutta—two nights and a day on the same plane. We would join Charlie and Gay in Japan.

The flight from Calcutta to Bagdogra took only an hour and a quarter. The airport there was being enlarged as part of India's defenses against the Chinese, who were threatening Sikkim. The latter country is under Indian protection.

There were a dozen cars drawn up in a line, each flying the flag of a different country. These were the ambassadors' cars. There was no car for us. The Sikkimese representative was most apologetic. "You are supposed to have a car but there aren't enough cars." He offered us our choice between a jeep to ourselves or a ride in a bus with a dozen others, mostly press and photographers. We chose the bus. We knew that it had been raining steadily for three days and three nights in Sikkim and there were ominous dark clouds over the mountains. The jeeps had only canvas curtains.

The date of the coronation, April 4, 1965, had been selected by the Buddhist priests as being auspicious. As the day drew near, the rains started. The world's best meteorologists predicted the rains would not cease until April 5. The Buddhist lamas put teams of non-rain-making monks to work praying in shifts around the clock for clear weather. We had been told in Calcutta that they had never failed.

On the short trip from Bagdogra to the border we were fascinated by the thousands of Indian soldiers quartered in tents under tall trees on either side of the road. There were thousands of vehicles drawn up in neat rows—mostly trucks and jeeps. We did not see any big guns.

Soon we started to climb. The road was narrow and winding and our driver had to blow his horn at every turn— usually every one hundred yards or less. If we met a car or truck one of us would stop and somehow the other would edge by. In many places part of the road had slid into the valley below and what was left was particularly narrow and dangerous. It was a little disconcerting when on one particularly hazardous curve our driver leaned his head out of the window and spat down a thousand feet.

Luckily the scenery was so beautiful that we were distracted from watching the road. Soon we were in the rain forest. Orchids of every variety were growing in the tall trees. There were massive rhododendrons but unfortunately they were not yet in bloom. We enjoyed the bamboo trees and the ferns.

We saw only a few people along the road. Practically all the traffic in both directions was army traffic. For a while we followed a wild and beautiful river, crossing it occasionally. When we came to a bridge decorated with prayer scarves, we knew we had come to Sikkim—a country the size of Yellowstone Park.

We showed our "Inner Line" passes and were soon on our way. Darkness fell and fortunately traffic diminished to almost nothing. There were fewer curves in the road but we were still climbing.

We were not prepared for our first view of Gangtok, the capital of Sikkim. We rounded a corner and there high above us and ahead was a gaily illuminated mountaintop. It was like seeing Hong Kong at an elevation of 4,000 feet—but not as many lights, of course. Winding down from the city was a tail of lights. The last couple of miles, as the road approaches the city, there were widely spaced street lights.

We went to a well-organized reception center where we were given our supervisor and a jeep to take us to our quarters.

Our room was large, with a good-sized bathroom. Before we had finished unpacking a servant arrived with glasses, ice and five different kinds of alcoholic drinks. Dinner was sent over from the palace and was hot and delicious.

When we awoke the morning of the coronation, we knew

the monks had prevailed. It was a beautiful day. We were told that if it had rained, the lamas were prepared to announce that they had prevented a bad hail storm.

The sky was dark blue with just a few puffs of white clouds for contrast. During the night the Himalayas had been freshly powdered with new snow for the occasion. Towering over all was the third highest mountain in the world, Kanchenjunga.

Out of our bedroom windows we could see the nearby majestic mountains, terraced with rice paddies. Just below us and to our right were several beautiful buildings with convex overhanging roofs painted a beautiful bright blue with just a touch of green in the color. In the distance we could see the winding road we had traveled in darkness the night before.

For the first time in my life I had breakfast in my cutaway at seven-thirty in the morning. Then Mary appeared in her coronation finery.

She had been told in New York—incorrectly, as it turned out—that she was to wear a full-length evening dress and a hat! She had bought a new Dior creation for the occasion. It was black with large geometric blotches of bright colors. Her hat was a shocking pink turban. She looked like a combination of Aunt Jemima and a gypsy fortuneteller.

Walking in and out of the temple and mingling with the crowds, she was a sensation. The newly crowned King was familiar to them but they had never seen anything like this apparition from the West. The children followed her in crowds that would have made the Pied Piper look like the Long Ranger. Their laughter was natural and friendly.

The Sikkimese believe that laughter floats up to heaven, is frozen, and becomes a star. In one day, Mary created a whole new Milky Way.

About a hundred yards above our guest house we could see a row of gay flags. A winding road led upward toward them. Along this road the people of Gangtok had been trudging since daylight. Their various costumes for the occasion fascinated us.

Our car was waiting and we drove up the road out onto a flat plateau on top of the hill. Nearby was the beautiful red and gold temple, and in the distance, the royal palace. The "troops" were drawn up in lines in an open field. They consisted of about seventy-five red-coated soldiers, a bagpipe band and Boy and Girl Scouts. The latter were dressed in marine blue jumpers. There were many colorful flags and banners.

It made a beautiful sight against the dark green foliage, the white snow in the distance and the blue sky overhead.

The crowds would see the coronation on closed circuit television produced by BBC. We were among the fortunate two hundred-odd who had been assigned seats in the temple. These turned out to be in the fifth row, directly in the middle, so we saw everything to perfection.

The temple was ornately decorated with intricate carvings. The predominant colors were gold, red and white. On our right against the wall were two rows of lamas in robes of cinnamon, magenta, scarlet and gold. They wore tall peaked hats and held banners and ceremonial umbrellas.

We had hardly settled in our seats when we heard the rolling of the great monastery drums. We knew it was 9:22 A.M. the moment deemed auspicious by the lamas. The royal couple emerged from the palace and walked to the temple on a red carpet lined on either side by the "troops." Behind them were massed the people of Gangtok.

The lamas struck up weird music on strange instruments as the royal pair entered and seated themselves on their thrones. The Gyalino's was slightly lower than that of the Choygal's. He was dressed in saffron and gold and she wore a red gown with a pearl and diamond diadem on her head.

The ceremony lasted about an hour and a half. It involved

recitations, prayers, offerings of food and incense. At the end there were several speeches followed by the presentation of scarves and gifts. The family came first and each member bowed four times and offered a scarf first to the Choygal and then to the Gyalino. Then came government officials followed by other Sikkimese. These were followed by ambassadors and others from all over the world.

Some of the gifts were fabulous—bolts of Chinese and Russian brocades, incense, bags of grain, jade bowls, vessels of silver and gold, jewels, and even a sheep with a ribbon in a bow at its throat.

Then came our turn. We stepped forward laden down with (1) two cameras; (2) two scarves; (3) two presents. There is a protocol way of presenting the scarves. They are wound up tight but a pull with the left hand releases them so that you can drape them over your hands held far apart in front of you. The Choygal extended his two arms and Mary placed her scarf on top of those he was already holding. She repeated the performance for the Gyalino. Not easy to do with a camera, presents and purse.

I followed Mary. The Gyalino murmured, "Why didn't you two come earlier?" and extended her arms for the scarf. I was about to shake her outstretched hand when I remembered protocol and clumsily presented my scarf.

We left the temple and mingled with the crowds. There was so much to photograph—natives in their rough homespun or Tibetan cloaks contrasted with women in beautiful Indian saris or Paris fashions, or the marvelous gowns of Bhutan. There were men in top hats and women with jeweled headdresses.

But there was nobody dressed like Mary. I wished I could have gotten a picture of her with the Head Lama, who is known as the "Red Hat Lama." The belief is that if left to itself, his red hat would fly up to heaven. Therefore, he always keeps one hand on his hat, or otherwise two men walk beside him holding on his hat.

Before lunch we went home to our guest cottage and I changed out of my cutaway and Mary gave up trying to frighten evil spirits away.

A buffet luncheon was served in the largest tent I have ever seen outside of a circus. The top was of some sort of temporary construction and only the sides were of canvas. There were several large bars and a number of buffet tables with all the delicious food you would find at a fashionable wedding at home. We understood everything was trucked up from Calcutta.

After lunch, Mary and I took a tour of Gangtok and visited two markets. They were a good deal cleaner than most of those we had seen in Asia and Africa, and we were amazed at the good-looking fresh vegetables and fruit since we had seen nothing but rice paddies and tea plantations.

At four-fifteen, we went to see some folk dances in the local school auditorium. The costumes were interesting, but the dances too long and repetitious.

Dinner was in the same pavilion as luncheon. While I was lapping up a few drinks at the bar, the Gyalino came over and said, "You had better eat in a hurry as there are so many gate crashers the food is running out."

The buffet was Chinese and eaten with chopsticks. I am not too bad with the latter when the plate is on a table but when I have to balance it while standing up, I am out of my class.

Fortunately I was not put to the test. When I wanted to eat there were no plates and no chopsticks left—and very little food. I settled for a ball of uncooked dough with some kind of meat inside.

There was a dance after dinner on a very good temporary dance floor and a marvelous orchestra from Calcutta. Even I was fascinated by the myriad beautiful and exotic gowns worn by the women of all nations. Some of the jewels were fabulous.

The party was to go on all night but we had to leave at

3:00 A.M. to catch our plane from Bagdogra to Calcutta and thence to Tokyo.

We caught an hour and a half's sleep, dressed groggily and climbed into our car. It was ice cold with no heat and spring comes late in the Himalayas. I returned to our bedroom and took two luxurious blankets off the Royal Guest House bed, leaving a note that the driver would bring them back.

The return trip to Bagdogra was much easier than our trip up. We had a car to ourselves instead of an uncomfortable bus, there was no traffic, and we were going down, not up. We tried to doze in the darkness but we were too cold so talked instead. We reviewed the events of the last two days. When we came to the dance we recalled the incredible incident that happened to us at President Eisenhower's first Inaugural Ball.

Mary had been co-chairman with Walter Williams of Citizens for Eisenhower, both before and after his nomination for President. As a result, the Lords and the Williamses were given a box for six at one of the balls the night before Eisenhower became President.

Our son Winston was allowed time off from the Hotchkiss School as the headmaster thought it would be a good educational experience for him. The Williamses had invited a friend.

When the six of us went to our box, we found two of the chairs occupied by two elderly ladies in their seventies. They were dressed in their turn-of-the-century finest, complete with feathered boas. Their high cheekbones were dabbed with too much too-red rouge. They reminded us of the "Whoops Sisters" created by my classmate, the late Peter Arno, in the early days of *The New Yorker* magazine.

They obviously had no intention of moving, so Winston and I balanced ourselves on the box rail.

One of them noticed me eyeing her rather strange evening

purse. It was a covered straw basket about six by twelve inches and four inches high. It reminded me of the basket in which I used to take my snack for recess at Miss Hall's Kindergarten.

She turned to me and said, "Would you like to see what I have in the basket?" and thereupon opened it to reveal a small turtle!

Before we recovered from our surprise she said, "Would you like to see the turtle wave the American flag?"

We were too speechless to reply, but she produced a tiny American flag anyway. When she put it in one of the turtle's feet, it grasped it and waved it vigorously.

Our box was directly below that of Vice-President and Mrs. Nixon's. We knew the TV cameras would be on them and hoped they did not pick up the incident in our box. Our viewing friends would probably have assumed that the two ladies were our mothers and that at least one of them was a little balmy.

After these reminiscences we fell into a fitful sleep but roused ourselves at daylight as we did not want to miss anything. We might never be back.

I remembered Sir Thomas More's lines with which I have usually agreed:

> And the best of all ways
> To lengthen our days.
> Is to steal a few hours from the night, my dear.

The early morning sun was slanting through the tall trees. The light was golden, not yellow, and the shadows sparkled with frost.

Mary asked me, "Who was it said, 'For the Lords a yawn takes the place of a good night's sleep'?"

We could not remember.

We both yawned.

17

"Do You Know What Kind of Works a Big Tree Doing?"

FROM BAGDOGRA we returned to Calcutta. The city is depressing enough in daytime with its million homeless people. We saw it under even worse circumstances. At five in the morning we motored to the airport for our flight to Tokyo through what in any other city would be deserted streets. These were populated by the living dead. Every block had thirty or forty figures sleeping on the sidewalks—a lucky few had straw mats. I remonstrated with our driver when he blew his horn needlessly. Why waken these poor wretches to another day of nothing?

We were met at the Tokyo airport by Mr. Morio, a driver guide that Mary's brother, Phil Pillsbury, had had the year before. We were at first confused on our way into the city when he kept referring to a "Mr. and Mrs. Rord." It finally dawned on us that he was referring to our son Charlie and his wife Gay, who had arrived a day before us. He had even more difficulty than most Japanese in pronouncing the letter "L."

After a few days we learned to understand him and I had no difficulty in knowing what he meant when he announced plans one morning: "Mr. Rord you have exerrent runch in rittle virrage arongside rittle rake at ereven hundred feet erevation."

Tokyo is a sprawling, characterless, garish, uninteresting city. We spent very little time there. Instead we motored to see the various shrines and temples of which we had heard so much and many of which I had visited in 1927. They were overrun with Japanese sight-seeing tours composed almost entirely of elderly people. They shuffled two abreast behind leaders with placards carrying numbers ranging as high as eighty. When one group had been dutifully photographed before a shrine, another group would take its place. Though there might be only three or four contingents in line for their pictures, there were often a dozen or more swarming around the shrines. The presence of these disciplined mobs inevitably detracted from our enjoyment of the scene.

We preferred the gardens to anything we saw in Japan. We visited a great many of them but the one we preferred was the moss garden at Kokedera. It was particularly beautiful —acres of delicately textured "velvet" in a thousand tints of green, interspersed with beautifully shaped and carefully selected rocks. There were little streams and a dozen stone bridges. The soft light filtering through the tall trees enhanced the quiet beauty of the garden.

The Japanese use of rocks revealed to us a new vista of beauty that has to be seen—not described. We were familiar with the carefully chosen ones surrounded by meticulously raked white gravel. Not so familiar were the different shaped textured and colored rocks carefully and artistically placed under trees, in little streams or ponds or encircled in soft moss.

Spring in Japan was very late in 1965. The hotel keepers were desperate for cherry blossoms. We did not realize how concerned they were until we read a triumphant sign next to the elevator in the Fujuja Hotel in Kyoto one night:

"Cherry Blossom is started to bloom. It can be seen from opposite window of 763 on the Seventh Floor."

We rode up to the seventh floor but had a little difficulty locating "opposite window of 763."

There it was! A Japanese cherry blossom in bloom! We recognized it instantly from the thousands of paper cherry blossoms strung across the streets, decorating restaurants and in every shop window.

We saw more cherry blossoms a week later, when motoring in the south. They are pretty but we decided that the emphasis the Japanese put upon them brings most tourists to their country at the wrong time. Even if the season had not been late, the countryside is not at its best at cherry blossom time.

The hotels and inns in Japan we found excellent. The Western style ones have the best service in the world. The Japanese style ones were equally good but a little confusing. We sought them out and enjoyed them though I found their customs a little baffling. I always seemed to have the wrong things on my feet.

I recall the first evening we spent the night in a Japanese-type hotel. We left our shoes just inside the front door. We were supplied with slippers which we were permitted to wear as far as our bedroom door. There a dainty little Japanese girl laid down the ground rules. I listened carefully and followed them more or less correctly the first time. I removed my slippers, stepped up three inches and walked in stockinged feet across the main room covered with tatami mats.

Then I stepped down to a little room where another pair of slippers awaited me to replace the ones I had left five steps behind. The new ones were beginning to feel comfortable and cozy when I had to remove them after two steps. I could not go out on the balcony without another change of footwear.

Returning, I changed back again to the cozy ones, took two steps to the right and put on the special slippers worn in the bathroom.

After this first trial run, I never seemed to perform the ritual properly. We therefore evolved our own system as we moved from one Japanese hotel to another. Mary would sit cross-legged on the floor between the Japanese flower arrangement and the TV set and call signals.

The slippers had only toe straps. As a result when I stepped backward they often did not accompany me.

Taking a bath was also quite a ritual. You fill the tub with water but do not climb in right away. Instead, you sit on a little stool near a water tap where you fill a plastic bucket. You slosh the water over yourself, soap, and then pour several more buckets over your head. When properly cleansed, you may step into the tub. The plug of the latter is never pulled by any one but the maid.

It was not until our second bath experience that Mary assured me that I was permitted to remove my pink plastic bathroom slippers in the tub.

The first requirement in a Japanese style inn is to remove your European clothing at the first opportunity. In spite of stories that we had heard about Japanese maids undressing you, Charlie and I always removed our own pants.

Men and women change into similar clothes. First you don a cotton kimono and over that a woolen one tied with a sash.

There are no dining rooms in the inns. All meals are eaten in the bedrooms. We alternated each night between our room and Charlie's and Gay's. The cooking as well as the serving was always done right in the rooms by one and sometimes two diminutive pretty Japanese maids.

We sat on the floor around a very low table. Charlie and I had trouble with our legs. He is six feet four.

Our favorite dinner was sukiyaki. The beef was very tender and sliced very thin. It was cooked on the table with butter, soy sauce, pea pods, bamboo shoots, etc. We ate with chopsticks. As fast as we emptied our tiny glasses the maids would fill them again with properly warmed sake.

We slept on the floor. The thin mattresses were usually very hard, so we developed the habit of sleeping between the two heavy comforters instead of pulling both over us.

It is harder to do as the Japanese do than do as the Romans do.

Several times we traveled by train and found Japanese trains as good as they were reputed to be. Each passenger had a comfortable swiveled seat and food and drinks were served on individual tables. The whole train was swept clean at each stop. Lemons were freshly squeezed for our whiskey sours. We remembered the New Haven Railroad as we enjoyed the novelty of looking at the countryside through clean windows—not "as through a glass darkly."

The boats on the Inland Sea were just as good. One, a catamaran, even had a Japanese garden on the broad deck amidships.

Having read so much about the scarcity of land in Japan, we expected to find the hillsides extensively terraced. Actually, most farming was done on level ground and plastic coverings were widely used. We never learned whether poor soil or lack of irrigation was the reason for the sparse use of hilly country. It was in sharp contrast to countries like Nepal and Indonesia where nearly every foot of land is utilized.

We learned that the traditional Japanese courtesy had its drawbacks. When we told our travel agent that we preferred a 3:30 P.M. train to a 5:00 P.M. one he obligingly changed our tickets accordingly. The train left at 5:00 P.M.

We found that when in doubt the Japanese giggle.

The use of house paint is almost unknown in Japan.

The Japanese wrap all packages in pieces of cloth, never paper. Even if they have a box, instead of carrying it as such or putting a string around it, they tie it up in a handkerchief or scarf and hold it by the knot.

After Charlie and Gay left us to go on around the world by way of Hong Kong (we were going through Siberia), Mary and I flew to the large northern island of Hokkaido and landed at Sapporo.

The city was laid out in American style in 1870 when the Japanese asked President Grant to send over some American experts to develop the island. Sapporo looks like a Western American city of about 1890 and could be the scene of any TV Western if it were not for the Japanese lettering on the signs. There was nothing to see in the city so we persuaded our new Japanese guide to take us to our inn at Jozankei for luncheon and not wait until late afternoon as originally scheduled. This took some doing. Once a Japanese has been given instructions he tries to follow them to the letter.

Except for this quality, our guides were excellent, particularly a Mrs. Hara, who had been recommended to us. Our guide on Hokkaido proved to be the exception. After three days, we decided he was a kindergarten dropout from a school for the mentally retarded.

We of course had heard a great deal about the Japanese custom of men and women bathing naked together. We had decided it was not for us.

After luncheon at Jozankei, I passed the communal bath and thought I should see what one looked like.

As I opened the door an attractive young girl with a good figure strolled by. She was completely nude except for a small washcloth which she used like a fig leaf. She held it

delicately in her left hand with her little finger extended—
the way one holds a crumpet at an English tea party. Such
modesty is not considered cricket in the best Japanese bathing circles.

I decided that my attitude toward communal bathing had
been too negative and that I should take a more positive
approach. I convinced Mary that we should not visit Japan
without taking a typical bath.

We went down to the basement in our kimonos about six
o'clock. We had separate dressing rooms. Mary was alone in
hers but I shared mine with several men. After shedding
everything, I sucked in my stomach, squared my shoulders,
threw out my chest, took a deep breath and stepped through
the door to the "arena." I felt like an early Christian martyr
entering the Colosseum.

At the same moment Mary appeared looking like Botticel-
li's Venus, except that her neck was straight.

We were relieved to find the steam was so thick it was
like a heavy fog. Directly ahead and to the left was what
looked like a horse's watering trough. It was encircled with
a six inch high gutter full of water and nearby were half a
dozen plastic buckets.

I grabbed a bucket and stepped forward to dip up some
water from the waist-high basin. As I did so I put one foot
in the water in the gutter. The attendant shrieked in horrified dismay. I had goofed again. No feet in the water!

Since I could not reach the watering trough without stepping in the water, I sloshed myself with water from the
gutter. After we had both soaped and rinsed we strode
determinedly toward the communal pool—about twenty by
twelve feet. Fortunately it was empty of other people. We
sat on the edge and dangled our feet in the very hot water.
When we had gotten used to that we slid forward and sat on
a shelf in about a foot of water. When we were boiled
lobster-pink to the waist we sat on the floor of the pool in
water up to our necks.

A casual glance around did not reveal the girl I had seen at lunch time. Through the steam we could see the rear view of half a dozen naked bodies—sex unknown. There was another dunking pool beyond but there was too much "fog" to see who was in it.

We had our pool to ourselves and later went downstairs and swam in the eighty by twenty foot swimming pool. Here the water was only tepid. It was only three feet deep so I was glad I did not use the diving board. Again this time we had the pool to ourselves.

We motored on to Lake Toya, where our room faced the water. It was a large room with eight tatami mats. All tatami mats have the same dimensions: six by three feet. Rooms are measured by tatami mats, not feet or yards.

Wearing slippers on a tatami mat is like grounding your golf club in sand.

We were startled by the view from our window. Across the lake, the setting sun glowed on a replica of Mt. Fuji-yama. I was so excited at this unexpected scene that I ended up two moves away from my correct slippers.

The mountain before us was impressive but the one behind was unique. Though hundreds of feet high, it was only twenty-five years old. Its birth was shrouded in wartime secrecy. One day without warning, the crust of a farmer's field was broken by the thrust from below. Slowly and majestically, the subterranean world raised another observation post. After reaching its preordained altitude the docile volcano relaxed. It was still belching clouds of steam as a reminder of what might have been.

The next morning we took a trip on the lake. Besides the "skipper," there was a rather unusual deckhand handling the lines. She was dressed like an airline stewardess with spike heels three inches high. She did not have to worry about the miserably maintained deck.

We stopped at an island where there was a small museum

connected with forestry and lumbering. We were glad that
there were informative signs in English, such as:

"Do you know what kind of works a big tree doing?"

"Now listen what services do the forests make?"

"What structure has the wood?"

I flunked all three questions.

We motored the next day to Noboribetsu, which we were
told was a little like Yellowstone Park. The accent should
have been on "little."

In 1915 Father, Mother, four brothers, one sister and I
spent six days stage-coaching through Yellowstone behind
four horses. All I remember is the dust and the geysers.
They were a great deal more impressive than the holes hic-
cupping steam at Noboribetsu. The latter, however, were
often chosen by frustrated lovers as a way to commit suicide.

We were told the hot sulphur water baths were a great
cure. We had nothing to cure but our curiosity so we decided
to try another communal bath at the hotel that evening.

There was only one large dressing room for the men.
Baskets were stacked in one corner like trays in a cafeteria.
I took one for my clothes—two kimonos.

I had shed these before I noticed the men's dressing-room
attendant was a woman! Fortunately there was a large pillar
in the middle of the room. I tried to keep this between me
and the woman. Soon we were circling each other like a
couple of Japanese wrestlers except the post was between us.

When I escaped into the communal bath I found the steam
less concealing than in my previous experience. I looked
around for the pretty girl who had changed my ideas about
Japanese bathing customs. Maybe she was a tourist too. She
was not there. I would have recognized her—by her little
finger of course.

We flew back from Hokkaido and landed in a very dense
fog. Our first glimpse of the airstrip was from an altitude of
less than a hundred feet.

As we were gathering our things together, the Japanese stewardess announced over the loudspeaker system, "I hope you enjoyed your fright."

Motoring into Tokyo, we felt as though we were returning home. It was reassuring to read on a large signboard, "You have a Tomodachi at Chase Manhattan."

Mr. Morio reminded me "Mr. Rord your prane reaves tomorrow at ereven ocrock."

18

Yes Maybe, No But

In Tokyo we joined Phil Crowe, his daughter, Phillipa, John Hanes, Jr., and his wife, Lucy, for our planned trip through Siberia, Outer Mongolia and Russia.

We took a ship from Yokohama on Monday, April 26, 1965. It was the gayest sailing any of us had ever experienced. There were so many thousands of confetti streamers between dock and ship that for a moment I wondered if the *Baikal* would be able to break its paper fetters or be bound like Gulliver in Lilliput. It was a beautiful ship with the graceful lines we had admired on several Russian freighters we had seen in African ports. The *Baikal* was new. It was on either its first or second round trip from Novkorod to Yokohama. We never found out which. It would seem to be a simple easily answered question, and as far as we were concerned, immaterial.

This was our first experience with the Russian custom of never giving a straight answer to a straight question. It was always, "Yes maybe," or "no but."

We estimated there were probably several hundred passengers on board and at least three times as many to see them off—from the dock. They never had to announce "Visitors ashore, please."

The well-wishers were augmented by a large group of Japanese Communists who were there to wish the Red equivalent of "Godspeed" to a delegation of three of their number to the May Day celebration in Moscow. They were easily distinguishable by their large red banners.

They had their own cheerleaders on the dock but occasionally one of the three on board would take it upon himself to urge them on. When their enthusiasm lagged I cooperated by leading a few cheers myself. They were a little surprised, but good-natured. Everyone was having a good time and there was a holiday spirit in the air. It was as though a Princeton man led the Yale cheering section in the Bowl. The only difference was that I was sober.

Except for bar bills on the *Baikal* we seldom needed any form of currency in the U.S.S.R. We paid for everything in advance in New York. But not on the ship. There we paid for drinks in Japanese yen. The bar list quoted vodka at $1.11 a drink. Before lunch we had twelve of them and thought we would dispose of our yen. When I was sorting out our money the barmaid selected a 1,000 yen note worth $2.80 and gave me back some change. Maybe the abacus she was using was short a few beads.

We never did figure out the cost of drinks. We ran out of yen and paid in American money. No matter how many drinks we had, the bill was always one dollar. Vodka was the only alcoholic drink available. We never drank it straight but always with a little vermouth. The latter had been given to us as a bon voyage gift by our friends the Carney Laslies, who had been transferred from India to Japan. They also gave us two bottles of bourbon.

The two rather attractive barmaids were very good-natured. We taught them to make very decent vodka martinis. They were pleasant and friendly, in spite of the language barrier.

Our bedroom stewardess was clean and neatly dressed. She opened our stuck stateroom porthole the first day and we never saw her again. We made our own beds and emptied our wastebaskets overside.

My first breakfast on the *Baikal* was rather a shock. Instead of fruit juice I was given a glass of milk. I did not care if it was cow's milk, camel's milk or yak's milk but I had not figured on buttermilk. I had drunk it once before late at night when some saboteur had sneaked it into the family refrigerator. That time it never got past my tonsils.

This time I realized instinctively that the honor of my country was at stake. I gagged down the buttermilk and picked up a cold hard-boiled egg from a plate in front of me. When I cracked it to peel the shell some of the yolk splattered on my lap. I had never seen a half-minute cold soft-boiled egg before. I decided to take the chill off another one and dunked it in my tea for several minutes. It came out looking like a tan Easter egg. It was the same color as the bread and the tap water in our stateroom.

The dining room service was quick and efficient. We ordered our luncheons and dinners a day in advance by numbers on the menus, which were in English as well as Russian, and several other languages. Most of the food was fried. It was not too bad, but the servings were teaspoon size. A Japanese whom we met on board and who had traveled on Russian ships before, advised us not to make a choice but take one of everything. His advice came too late.

The first night there was a gala in the lounge. The six-piece Russian orchestra was very good. The band leader

made an announcement that we, of course, could not understand. When the first couple got out on the floor we decided
to give them "Hands across the sea" support and followed
suit. The music stopped. We had fouled up the floor show!

Everyone on board was very friendly and we spoke with
as many as possible in any mutual language we could manage.

After two days and two nights, we landed at Novkorod
late in the afternoon. It is near Vladivostok, but no one is
allowed at the latter port because it is a naval base. The
Russian customs officials were polite and efficient. Instead of
waiting in line as in entering the United States, we sat in
our stateroom until the officials arrived to make a perfunc-
tory examination of our luggage.

On the dock there was a large delegation of school children waving red banners. They were apparently there to
welcome the Japanese Communist delegation. We were the
first off the ship. As we started down the gangway we waved
and smiled at the kids. They broke ranks and crowded
around us presenting us with flowers and souvenirs that we
guessed were intended for our three Japanese shipmates. In
return, we gave them anything we could find in our pockets
or the girls' purses. Our gifts ranged from crushed paper
cherry blossoms to individual Alka-Seltzers in their blue foil.

We boarded a waiting bus and the children gathered
around, pressing gifts upon us. Many took little medals off
their clothes and insisted upon our taking them. It suddenly
dawned upon us that perhaps they had *not* made a mistake.
None of us looked Japanese. Maybe they were trying to
express the friendship for Americans that we found everywhere in Siberia.

It was only a few hundred yards to the waiting train and
many of the children followed us. When I had settled our
baggage, I returned to the station platform. I was not too
surprised to see Mary and John Hanes playing blindman's

buff with the kids. If they noticed Mary cheating by taking an extra step they were too polite to say so. I hoped they did not put it down as a normal manifestation of the free enterprise system.

Stewardesses in navy blue uniforms and clean white gloves stood by the steps of the *wagon-lit* cars. As the train pulled out we saw them climb aboard and pull up the steps. We never saw them again. We made and unmade our berths as we had on the *Baikal*. We were beginning to understand why Russia calls itself the "Workers' Paradise." A lot of the workers were not working very hard.

Our staterooms were small but adequate. Instead of our having three together we had every other one. It just happened that the two alternate rooms were occupied by Russians who understood English perfectly. In one was our Intourist guide and in the other a very young, attractive and vivacious girl whom we nicknamed "Mata Hari."

After dinner we invited her into our compartment. She was fun and we all enjoyed ourselves killing one of the two bottles of bourbon the Laslies had given us along with the vermouth.

The next morning my tea was too cold to take the chill off my half-minute egg. I did not care too much as I was busy observing the countryside. We were passing through the tundra. It was flat and bare with puddles of water in many places. There were only a few shacks grouped in very small villages at intervals along the railroad. There were no houses in the distance. A miserable road of two weed-infested ruts connected the villages. Between 8 and 11 A.M. I saw one truck and one horse-drawn cart on this road. The Chinese border was only a few miles away.

By noon the scenery changed. There were more trees, many of them birch. They had a silvery glow in the sunlight and were very pretty against the brown hills that were beginning to close in on us. One line of birches at the base of a symmetrical brown hill looked like a graying fringe of hair below a sunburned bald pate.

We arrived at Khabarovsk early in the afternoon. Through some bureaucratic blunder, we were put in separate hotels a mile apart—the Crowes and Haneses in the local "Waldorf," and Mary and me in a "Times Square Hotel." We thought this unimportant until at cocktail time when we faced a crisis. We had the vermouth and they had the vodka!

We had time our first afternoon to walk about Khabarovsk. It is a dull, colorless city with wide streets and clean sidewalks. For the first time we realized how few automobiles there are in Russia. Long avenues would be devoid of any traffic for minutes at a time. Trucks outnumbered passenger cars. We were told that most of the latter belonged to party officials or were taxis. There were not even many bicycles.

The Natural History Museum was officially closed but was obligingly opened for us because of Phil and John's status in the wildlife field. The director was a charming, gracious, bearded man with a nice smile and crinkles about his eyes. He was impressed with our friends' knowledge and they, with a mounted tiger of a species practically extinct, and a rare leopard.

We walked through the spacious park bordering the Arnu River. The few people we met were smiling and friendly. They recognized us immediately as Americans and tried their grammar school English on us.

That night we merged our vermouth and vodka in the "Waldorf" Hotel. It was a gay evening with the young Russians dancing to American jazz. Philippa Crowe was the belle of the international ball.

We had wanted to continue on by the Trans-Siberian railroad from Khabarovsk to Irkutsk but that was forbidden as that was the countryside where rockets were tested and launched. We therefore flew.

When we weighed in all our luggage together for our flight we were told we were thirty-seven pounds overweight. Phil Crowe said, "Of course we are overweight. What did you expect? We are capitalists." We did not pay anything extra.

Our plane was crowded with more than a hundred passengers who shared one common dirty lavatory. There was no pressurization but the lunch was passable.

All foreigners regardless of nationality share a special Intourist lounge in Russian airports. Since we were the only non-Russians on our flight, we had the place to ourselves in Irkutsk—for thirty seconds. Then the police arrived to take John Hanes before a tribunal of three for questioning. Phil insisted on going along as leader of our "Expedition." I stayed with the three girls and we all wondered what was wrong.

There was never any doubt in our minds that the Russians knew the background of our party. Phil had been U.S. ambassador to Ceylon and South Africa; John Hanes, Jr., in the State Department in charge of Security, and Mary, eight years at the United Nations.

After an anxious half hour, John and Phil returned, smiling, and explained the difficulty. We had been assured we could photograph anything but bridges and airports, so John had innocently taken a picture of frozen Lake Baikal from ten thousand feet. The soldier sitting next to him never tried to stop him but reported the incident on arrival.

After some discussion before the tribunal, John opened his camera and double exposed the last few pictures and everything was forgiven.

Our guide in Irkutsk was a very intelligent man whose name began with "L," and since we could not pronounce it, we simplified matters by calling him "Lenin."

After he deposited us at the Siberia Hotel, Mary went for a walk alone and had her first frustrating experience marketing in Russia. Seeing a large grocery store, she decided to try to buy some fresh fruit so we could start the day right. She queued up in the fruit and vegetable line, with her eye on the last three oranges. They were still there when she arrived at the head of the line. Her triumph was short-lived.

The clerk told her the cost of the three oranges but said she must present a paid-up receipt before she could have them.

Mary went back to the line at the cashier's desk. In ten minutes it was her turn. She purchased the three ruble ticket and stationed herself for the second time at the end of the fruit and vegetable line, which had grown longer. Twenty minutes later when she presented her three ruble receipt, she found someone had beaten her to the last three oranges. Since her receipt was not refundable and all the lines were equally long, she decided to turn in her slip for anything available.

I do not recommend raw onions for breakfast.

"Lenin" was an interesting man who spoke much more freely than most Russians. He told us he received one hundred and fifty rubles a month and paid only ten rubles monthly for a one-room apartment with bathroom and kitchenette. The rent included water and electricity. He had a wife but no children. We had him and his wife for dinner one night.

He said most families lived on bread, lard, potatoes and fish. The latter are cheap but he did not like them. Beef was expensive and chicken even more so. A decent suit cost one hundred and fifty rubles—a month's salary.

Our second day in Irkutsk was May 1, the Reds' May Day. We had been given tickets for "podium seats" and we looked forward to the parade. We walked to the reviewing stand, leaving our hotel by the back door as the front door was locked to keep the crowds out of this vantage point on the parade route.

Mary was appropriately dressed for the occasion. She wore an enormous bright red beret, bigger than a large pizza—more like a small flying saucer.

Our "podium seat" tickets permitted us to stand on the sidewalk near the reviewing stand. The dignitaries there also stood—there were no chairs. We were glad to roam around as we could see more and get better pictures. The people were very nice to us and kept urging us to get in the front row.

The first twenty minutes of the parade were interesting. No soldiers or weapons. Platoons of young men and girls going through calisthenics in unison as they marched—floats with tiers of gymnasts performing as they rolled along. It reminded me of pictures Winston had taken in the Moscow Stadium several years earlier.

Then came groups carrying flowers—all I think artificial —a daisy group, an apple blossom group, a lily of the valley group, etc. There was even a Forest Conservation group, conserving by carrying real "Christmas trees." It looked like Burnham Wood going over to spend a weekend at Dunsinane.

The parade soon disintegrated into a shuffling mass of humanity. Families trudged by in groups, the mothers holding their children's hands and the fathers carrying the babies on their shoulders.

After forty-five minutes we had all seen enough—except Mary and John Hanes. We other four decided to return to our hotel. It was almost impossible to move on the crowded sidewalks. We decided there was only one solution—join the parade.

No uniforms were necessary. Each contingent represented the workers of one factory. They had "volunteered" to march in the parade. We joined a group from a tractor factory and marched merrily along smiling and shaking hands with our good-natured fellow workers in paradise.

When we reached our Siberia Hotel we had trouble getting out of the parade. Apparently, once you have volunteered for the parade you are expected to go the whole way. We were forced back in line by several men in uniform before they realized we were tourists.

Meanwhile, the director of the local radio station asked John Hanes to broadcast over it. He did so and was translated sentence by sentence, speaking about wildlife conservation. He was too polite to express his opinion of the bear hunts carried on by the French with the cooperation of some Russian hunters. When one of the latter finds a hole where a bear is hibernating for the winter, he notifies the appropriate person in Moscow, who wires the "Hunter Group" in Paris. The next French "hunter" on the waiting list pays fifteen hundred dollars and flies out to Siberia. He is then led to the hole and the poor bear is prodded out with sticks. Still blind with sleep, he is shot on the spot.

That night we enjoyed the circus in its permanent building. The show was excellent and the lion act far superior to any I have ever seen. We could not understand Russian but we gathered that the clowns were very witty. I use the word advisedly as they were more like night club comedians than the clowns to which we were accustomed. The intimacy of one ring made it possible to hear every word without distractions.

One of the reasons for Phil Crowe's planning a trip to Siberia was to check on the status of the fresh water seal. Twenty years earlier they were reported to have been reduced in numbers to about three thousand. Their habitat was Lake Baikal.

We motored for several hours to the shore of the lake, which was still solidly frozen though it was early May. Baikal is the largest fresh-water lake in the world. Four hundred miles long and three miles deep, it contains a volume of water greater than our five Great Lakes.

At the three-year-old Institute on the shore of the lake we spent several interesting hours with the assistant director. We believed her when she said the fresh water seals had been so protected that their number had increased to 60,000. She gave Phil enough information to substantiate her remarks.

The Institute, though small, was well worth visiting. We were particularly interested in the skeletons of fish brought up from the depths of Lake Baikal. These fresh water fish were strikingly similar to those from the same depth of salt water.

We were surprised to learn that there were sturgeon in Lake Baikal and that caviar was being shipped from there.

We spent a week altogether in Irkutsk. The Siberia Hotel was quite good and the food better than we were to find later in Moscow.

The city is a strange mixture of the very old and not so modern. The main street, Lenin Avenue, is wide and hard paved. One block away we found roads with mud more than a foot deep and pools of water in the depressions. Many of these streets were impassable to the few automobiles.

The old houses charmed us. Many of them were built of logs notched at the corners. Those that were made of wide wooden boards were the mellow brown color of weathered wood. There were carvings over every door and window and frequently on the eaves.

When walking alone one day, Mary was invited inside a house by a kindly white-haired woman who saw her admiring the flowers in the window. She was introduced to three generations of the family. Mary was able to explain to her that she too was a *Babushka* (grandmother) but was never able to get over the idea that she had twin grandsons. There was no running water or electricity in the house and only a wood stove for heating. That the latter was inadequate was shown by the strips of felt on the door jambs.

The government was building unattractive cell-like apartments with modern conveniences for the people but many of the older ones preferred staying where they were.

We enjoyed Irkutsk and were happy at the thought that we would have several more days there after our visit to Outer Mongolia.

19

May Is Springtime for Camels, Too

If you've never heard of Mongolia
Somebody should have tole ya
Niki and Nikita
Can't locate either
Perhaps a thought to console ya.

When I composed the above limerick in the time of Niki
Bulganin and Nikita Khrushchev, I never thought I would
ever be in Outer Mongolia.

Mary had come home from the United Nations one night
and said Outer Mongolia was applying for membership in
the UN. The U.S. delegation decided to treat the idea as
being ridiculous and Mary asked me if I could write a limerick to that effect. The above was the result.

Forty-eight hours later, at a reception for United Nations
delegates, three different men quoted the limerick to me. I
did not admit my authorship.

Our trip to Outer Mongolia was the result of a chance meeting in Washington between Mary and Phil Crowe. Phil mentioned that he, as one of the officers of the International Wildlife Foundation and John Hanes, Jr., as vice president of the Audubon Society, had obtained "difficult-to-secure" visas to travel in Outer Mongolia.

Mary phoned me at once, all excited, saying Phil thought he could get visas for us—even though we have trouble telling a duck from a canary. We have never been "bird watchers." I wonder if sometimes in their zeal to see a rare bird they don't miss the enjoyment of watching the commonplace ones around them. It seems to me a little like going to a large ball and trying to spot the Duchess of Windsor and overlooking the debutantes.

Our flight from Irkutsk to Ulan Bator took only a little over an hour. As we came down through the clouds we could see the camel-colored steppes below us. They were quite barren with a few small streams and occasional clusters of gers, the Mongolian name for yurts. These are the circular houses like tents that can be easily moved. In the distance were mountains with a little snow. They looked like jagged scoops of coffee ice cream with dabs of marshmallow whip on top.

We were amazed to find Ulan Bator such a modern city in many ways. There were dozens of new apartment buildings, four and five stories high. They were better-looking and seemed more substantially built than those in Siberia. Many of them were pastel colored, and the white ones had gaily colored balconies.

Our hotel surprised us. It was six stories high and a block long. Wide, red-carpeted stairways led upward halfway to the floor above—then they split right and left as in an opera house. On each floor, at the head of the stairs, there was a large reception hall furnished with modern Czechoslovakian furniture. The hotel was built by the Chinese when relations between the Mongolians and Chinese were more cordial.

Our English-speaking (?) Mongolian guide helped us register. Looking at the six of us, he asked John, "Would you like to share a room with your wife?" He replied, "In our country that is the usual custom." Later we learned that he meant to ask if a double bed would be all right.

Ulan Bator is not as modern as would appear at first sight. Seventy per cent of the 180,000 inhabitants still live in gers without most modern facilities. The government has enclosed these parts of the city with wooden fences to improve appearances.

The museum in Ulan Bator is astonishingly good and the temples gay and beautiful. Since there are no tourists in Outer Mongolia, we had them to ourselves—a welcome change from Japan, where the mobs detract so much from the shrines.

We found the Mongolians very much like the Nepalese, Sikkimese and Tibetan refugees—gay, smiling, friendly and good-natured. Our first night we were awakened by laughter, shouting and singing by hundreds of people in the square in front of our hotel rehearsing for a parade. It was like Times Square on New Year's Eve only it started at midnight instead of ending then. It lasted until 6:30 A.M. Occasionally a bus would arrive and a group would get out as another group got in. They were mostly children and teen-agers, but well behaved—just happy. They are so unsophisticated that they laugh and have a sense of humor and are not dependent on marijuana, LSD and pep pills as in more civilized countries.

On the third day we were told we were to motor fifty miles to see a workers' rest home. It didn't sound like a particularly fascinating objective but we wanted to see the countryside.

We took off in a twenty-seater bus—the six of us, "Dumbo"

as we had nicknamed our guide, and a smiling, pretty, apple-cheeked girl who was to be our cook and brought along food for us. We were not to share the food served up in the workers' paradise.

For the first half hour we had a two-lane, hard-surfaced road, then turned off to the left. The road was headed in the direction of the Chinese border but we were never able to find out how far it went.

Though there was practically no traffic, somehow two jeeps had managed to have a very bad head-on collision in the middle of a mile-long straight stretch of road just before we arrived at the scene of the accident. Except for the streets of Ulan Bator, this was the only road we saw in Outer Mongolia. The rest are ruts worn in the steppes or the Gobi. The countryside was pretty and rolling, with occasional gers and small herds of camels or cows, and a few sheep. There were fields of purple wildflowers like crocuses and yellow flowers like buttercups. "Dumbo" kept hurrying us every time we stopped for pictures, presumably so we wouldn't be late for lunch.

We were never shown the rest home that we had come to see except from a distance of several hundred yards. Instead, at twelve forty-five we stopped on a hill overlooking it in front of a row of five gers—one for cooking, one for eating, and three for sleeping. There was also an outhouse so new it had not yet been painted the traditional turquoise, which signifies, "For VIPs only." (In Mongolia, anyone who isn't a Mongolian is a VIP. They really want to please the very few outsiders who come to see their country.)

The rest camp had accommodations for about three hundred workers who get a month's vacation with pay every year. There was a bandstand and a dance floor of sorts but no other form of recreation that we could see.

After the usual meal of caviar, mutton, brown bread and cucumbers, we started our return trip. We had not gone far before we came upon what looked like an American Indian tepee of branches on end leaning on each other to form a conical shelter. Inside, a fire was burning. At first we thought meat was being roasted. Then we realized it was a funeral pyre. There were no mourners or any other persons in sight. The burning of bodies is a big improvement over the recent past when bodies were put outside for the wild dogs. One reason the wild dogs are so dangerous is because they have become fond of human flesh.

On our fourth day we were at the airport early for our eight o'clock departure and found several hundred people there and six planes. Apparently schedules were only approximate and no one seemed to know when a plane was to leave.

While waiting, we talked with a nice older Dutch woman who had just returned from a visit of several weeks alone in Red China. She said things were pretty bad there and she, of course, was only allowed to see the best.

I recalled the laughter of San San, Winston's Chinese sister-in-law, who spent her first seventeen years in Red China, when she read the account of a visit to a Chinese department store by an "authority" on China in one of his books. He wrote glowingly of the friendliness of the Chinese who crowded around him. "Of course," said San San, "when foreigners are in a store rationing is suspended and everyone takes advantage of the opportunity."

The ticket window in the airport reminded me of the old speakeasy days. It was about six inches square and every time it was opened I expected to see Matt Winkle, Dan Moriarty, or Jimmie of the Puncheon Club. Instead, it was an old crone. I never saw any business take place.

When a departure was announced, a horde would descend upon the plane. Then most would return. Visitors and those seeing friends off were definitely allowed beyond the gates.

We were told that our plane was the one with "Mongol

104" painted on the side. Though other planes departed sporadically, at 10 A.M. we were still waiting. When it was announced that there was engine trouble, we decided they probably saved the doubtful planes for the capitalists.

At ten-thirty we were told we would leave at one o'clock, and taken back to the hotel for an eleven-fifteen luncheon. We were glad in a way, as we saw the parade for which they had been rehearsing. It was by the Young Pioneers. Nice-looking, ruddy-cheeked, clean, neatly dressed little girls seemed to predominate.

We were back at the airport at twelve o'clock and found the plane had been repaired and the other passengers waiting for us. We were first aboard and sat near the back. "Dumbo" suggested that we move forward. We didn't, but for once he was right.

We no sooner took off before half the passengers were sick. Instead of the paper bags supplied by most airlines, the stewardess had one communal bucket. She would rush from one passenger to another, but always seemed to be between patients when the worst explosions took place.

Finally things were simplified and the bucket was placed in the open space at the back of the plane, next to our luggage! There three or four comrades could use it at once. Share and share alike.

Since we were in the next to last seat, Mary kept spraying cologne and the stewardess kept coming back for more of it. The latter was dressed in a silk, maroon-colored del tied with an orange sash. A del is like a kimono only the sleeves are normally not full. She wore a sheer bandana on her head.

We landed at Ur Hangar in a little over an hour but many of the sick passengers had to go on. There was no airstrip—just the steppes outlined with posts and lights. It was fenced to keep the animals out.

There were four jeeps awaiting us. The fourth one was for a cook with supplies. We started off at once as we had a six-hour trip before us, and it was now 2:15 P.M., not 9:15 A.M. as scheduled.

There were no roads, just tracks across the countryside. We started out four abreast, each driver to his own chosen ruts, but soon settled into a column with the jeeps about a quarter of a mile apart because of the dust. The ground was hard and flat and reminded us of the Serengeti Plain except there were no wild animals and no wildflowers. Also, the hills were quite nearby—not on or over the horizon as in Tanzania.

We had not gone more than a quarter of a mile when we passed two large demoiselle cranes strutting on our left. Occasionally we would pass a few whitened bones of some animal. There were very few signs of life and we would go for long periods of time without seeing a ger or anything moving. Several times we saw a lone rider on horseback. We saw a few camels, six or eight at a time, and an occasional flock of sheep.

The riding was rather rough, so we usually kept one hand on the bar on the back of the seat in front of us. Mary and I were on the back seat of the fourth jeep and had an Intourist man who supposedly spoke no English in the front seat with the driver. We believed he was also a security man.

After half an hour, our jeep broke down and the others disappeared over the horizon. There was no sign of habitation and the prospect of spending the night on the steppes didn't seem too inviting. We took inventory and found we had half a pound of chocolate and a bottle of vodka.

After fifteen minutes of hammering and tinkering, the jeep was fixed and we started in pursuit of the others.

We caught them at a small collective at five o'clock where "Dumbo" said we should stop for tea. Since we had only come 105 kilometers and had 120 more to go, we wanted to push on. But there is no changing a set program after some communistic bureaucrat has laid it out. Those down the line follow the orders of those higher up.

"Tea" was in a small restaurant. First we washed up. A girl poured water into a tin can with a hole in the bottom that was attached to the wall. Below this was a basin. We washed in the trickle that poured into it.

We were served a drink made of fermented milk of camels, goats and cows. It was like kurmiss but the latter is made of mare's milk alone. It was quite good and tasted like milk with champagne added. It did not taste sour.

The table was set as it was at every meal in Mongolia, breakfast, dinner and supper. There were several plates of mutton. It was sliced thin and in pieces about the size of Ritz crackers. There were the usual slices of cucumber, cheese and brown bread. Not too bad a repast, but monotonous. Also, the mutton might have been in better shape. The sheep are usually slaughtered in September. The meat keeps pretty well in the cold climate until spring. We were there in the middle of May!

In a few weeks the Mongolians would give up eating meat and switch to milk, cheese and milk products such as yogurt, until fall. The only vegetable we ever saw in Mongolia was cucumber. We never tasted fresh fruit or fruit juice and could find none in any of the markets or stores. In Ulan Bator we were able to purchase a can of strawberry jam. Not even canned fruit was available.

After our cold mutton and cheese, we were served a hot soup of mutton and noodles. This was followed by chopped-up mutton wrapped in a very heavy, sweet dough. This was tea!

We decided later that this was supposed to be our midday dinner, but we were late leaving Ulan Bator. Not even the menu could be changed—and besides "Dumbo" was, as usual, hungry.

After this unwanted delay of nearly an hour, we started out again. Soon we came over the crest of a hill and there, one hundred yards below us, was a large herd of camels—238 we learned later. It was a wonderful sight. They had come in off the steppes for the evening. There were many young ones among them.

They were making soft noises like the whine of babies. Mary was soon giving a very good imitation but I think she did not have it just right because before long she was being followed by about a dozen camels—all males. May is spring-time for camels, too.

The herdsman invited us into his ger and we each had a bowl of buttered tea. It was made of tea and camel's milk and flavored with salt and butter. There were also hard blocks of a camel's milk cheese. This was so sour that we followed our host's example and took a bite of a lump of sugar with each mouthful of cheese.

By eight-thirty we arrived at the cooperative where we were to spend the night. There were five special gers—one for each family, one for cooking, and one for eating. They were larger than most of those of the nomads—about twenty feet in diameter. Ours had two iron beds about twenty-seven inches wide—the width of a berth on a small boat. There was a cupboard, two low dressers, and a table.

There were two small foot-high stools with a basin on each. A woman came in with a kettle and poured half the con-tents in each bowl. I expected the water to be hot but it was ice cold. The nearest toilet was a four holer three hundred yards away. It had once been a bright blue and it didn't take just the shabbiness of the paint to convince us that it had been in use a long time.

We had the usual monotonous meal based on mutton. The canned small-grain caviar that the cook had brought along had turned a pale yellow and wasn't too palatable even with vodka.

Besides our five gers, there were about a hundred others, all alike. Coming home after a party at night must be like trying to find your own house in Levittown.

Gers have no windows so there is no spying on the neighbors. The circular walls are about four feet high and even the short Mongolians have to stoop to enter the narrow doorways. Back of the one-piece door there is usually another pair of doors, each half the width. The "ceiling" rises at a sharp angle to a hole in the middle. This is usually about four feet in diameter and is made of a concave "wagon wheel" which is open to the sky except for spaces between a few of the spokes which are covered with transparent plastic or glass. A cover can be pulled over the whole opening but usually a few sections are left open for light. There is also room for a stovepipe, which rises from the stove in the middle of the ger.

Seventy-five to a hundred gaily painted one and a half inch "beams" radiate from the wagon wheel to the sides of the ger. Over these and over the sides they stretch felt and cover the whole with white canvas. Three or four heavy ropes encircle the walls. The floor is made of boards and is usually covered with figured rugs, some fairly good. Inside around the walls there is a cotton skirt—usually green or blue.

In the cooperatives where there is a small generator, there is usually one small bulb hanging from the ceiling. In the isolated gers they use kerosene lamps. Only the outhouses for officials and guests are painted.

The next morning John Hanes got up a little after six to look for birds and photograph them with his very powerful telescopic lens. This was the chief reason for his being on our expedition. When he was about a mile from our little village a jeep drove alongside and two men gently but firmly eased him into it and drove him back to his ger. A little later when he had gone out again and was still near the village another jeep turned him back. After all, Outer Mongolia is a police state.

When John complained about this treatment, "Dumbo" said he was turned back because of the danger from wild dogs. None of us saw or heard a dog the whole time we were at the cooperative.

After breakfast we started out for the Gobi. The first hour we crossed the steppes with a few herds of sheep and camels in the distance. We also saw one small collection of gers and several wooden houses—obviously a cooperative of some sort.

To get to the Gobi we had to pass through the mountains. We followed the rocky bed of a dry river for about half an hour and then came out on the desert. It wasn't as different from the steppes as we had expected. There was no sand as in the Sahara or in the popular imagination. The land was flat and gravelly with little vegetaion, but with enough stubby weeds to feed camels.

We stopped for the usual meal of mutton, vodka and not much else by an almost dry steam, near a clump of bushes that could not have been more welcome, even if they had been turquoise blue.

After lunch we rode some camels from a nearby herd. The Mongolian camels are the Bactrian camels with two humps, unlike the one hump ones in India and Egypt, which are really dromedaries. When the Bactrian camels are healthy their humps stand erect. When they are sick, the humps flop over and hang limp like the breasts of old women in the Congo.

They are easier to ride than "dromedaries" because you fit snugly between the humps. They have a nasty habit of turning their heads around and braying in your face. They subscribe to the idea that halitosis is better than no breath at all.

On the way back to the mountain pass we stopped to visit a ger and had the usual buttered tea and sweet candies. The people were very hospitable and taught us how to milk a camel, not exactly a parlor trick.

Ours was the last jeep in line when our Intourist guide told our driver to head straight up a rather steep hill where there were no ruts. We came out on top of a ridge and could see the dust on the other jeeps below us to the right. We raced for miles along this narrow ridge with the land falling steeply on either side. The view for miles in every direction was very beautiful and we soon lost sight of the others behind us.

We dipped down to enter the mountain pass. We were three-quarters of the way through when we turned a sharp corner in the dry river bed. There two hundred yards ahead of us was a loaded camel caravan. It was as though no one had torn the pages off the calendar for a thousand years.

There were eight or nine camels, a family on the move. On the first camel sat a woman with a little child in front of her. There was another woman and child farther back and several men. The rest of the camels carried their household possessions. One had the circular top of a ger.

They plodded slowly and rhythmically on into the dark shadows of the pass and the past paying no attention to us or our cameras.

We drove on a few miles and stopped and waited for the others. Mary and I lay on the hard ground. From that perspective the barren steppe turned into a golden wheat field. The sparse growth seemed thicker and it was gilded by the reluctantly sinking sun. Suddenly on a nearby ridge appeared the black silhouettes of a man with two small children leading two horses—no woman in sight. When they finally disappeared over a small hill we were again alone on the endless, unchanging steppes. There was a chill in the air when the awaited jeeps emerged from the dark chasm that had been a sunlit pass in the morning.

After supper in our ger we saw a movie in the small community house of the cooperative. It was obviously put on for our benefit and was a treat for the ex-nomads. It was a propaganda film extolling the beauties of the Mongolian People's Republic and was quite well done.

We got an early start the next morning as we had to motor two hours beyond Ur Hangar, where our plane from Ulan Bator had landed. We wanted to make time but we had to stop for a camel milk break about ten-thirty because "Dumbo" was, as usual, hungry. While he ate a three course meal (mainly mutton) we visited the local store in the same town where we had had "tea" a few days before.

We were astounded at the prices. A pair of very poorly made children's shoes was $12.50. There were kerosene lamps, kettles, plain-colored piece goods, plates from Russia, toothbrushes, etc. The shop was so dark it was hard to see the various things displayed.

At Ur Hangar rooms had been reserved for us in the small hotel so we could take a rest. As it was then two o'clock, we wanted to have lunch and then push on. It was three-thirty before we had completed the slowly served meal. There was a further delay while a local dignitary read us a set speech in Mongolian. "Dumbo's" translation didn't exactly enthrall us.

When this was over we thought that at last we could get started. We were told that a show had been arranged for us and besides, we couldn't go because one of the jeeps had broken down. Every time our desires conflicted with bureaucratic planning a jeep broke down.

They were only trying to be hospitable and give us a good time. Some of the dancers and singers were excellent, so we didn't mind the delay. One tall stately girl in a white brocaded robe was outstanding.

It was a rough two-hour ride to Huijert; at one point we forded a stream so deep that we had to hold our feet off the floor, as it was two inches under water.

Huijert is a spa with hot sulphur springs. Maybe that was why there was no hot water in the bathroom. The toilet "paper" was a small pile of ragged pieces of thin cardboard.

The next morning we started out to see the country, a large waterfall, and do some fishing. We saw our first herd of yaks. They were mixed in with cows and there were many Hainags. The latter are a cross between a yak and a cow. Like mules, they don't figure in the population explosion— nor do they appear on the Mongolian emblem. The latter features the horse, the sheep, the goat, the camel and the cow (which includes the yak).

The nomads get their food and drink from these five animals and heat their gers by burning their dung. They don't need it for fertilizer because they grow very little.

We saw thousands of rodents sitting beside their holes. As we approached, they would pop underground. It reminded Mary of the gophers in her birth state of Minnesota. She broke into a school song of her youth which included lines like, "Gopherita Gopherota, we're the girls from Minnesota," and "We're all little gophers from the gopher state."

We forded some really large streams and in one, the second jeep got stuck. After a half hour's delay, the first jeep pulled it out with a rope. The others got across safely.

The falls were not very impressive, being only about 125 feet high and about 50 feet wide. We settled near them for a hot picnic cooked over an open fire. This time the mutton was ground up like hamburger and we had the luxury of a can of sardines. It soon started to snow and in no time, the ground was white.

After our "picnic" (it was too cold for ants), we went about a mile below the falls to fish. Our drivers used plugs and long "Yank 'em out" poles. They were curious and obviously disdainful, as John Hanes rigged a fly rod. It took him fifteen minutes to do so, and meanwhile they had not had a strike.

They watched with amusement that turned to awe when John made his first cast and caught an eighteen-inch grayling. He should have stopped then. In the next forty-five minutes neither he nor anyone else had a strike.

After our cold and wet day we were glad to get a hot bath

for the first time in nearly a week, even though we had to walk a quarter of a mile to the sulphur baths.

First we were ushered into a large room with a dozen low, long, white-painted tables with a block of wood at one end for a head rest. At first I thought I was in a morgue, until I saw one of the sheet-covered figures twitch.

Because the water is so hot, you are required to lie on one of these tables for twenty minutes before and after your bath.

After this experience and our usual mutton dinner, we were understandably sleepy and wanted nothing so much as to go to bed. Unfortunately, "Dumbo" had other ideas (or orders). We were to see a movie. If it was in our honor we naturally had to go. If it was a normal routine at the spa like Saturday night at the country club, we did not have to attend.

We never were able to find out so we decided we must go. We found the audience waiting for us and hoped we hadn't delayed them too long. "Dumbo" never told us ahead of time what we were to do, so we were frequently late for events that we never knew had been scheduled.

The next day we went to see the ruins of Karakorum, the capital of the immense empire conquered by Genghis Khan, who started his conquests in 1211. Today, there is nothing left but two large stone turtles and numerous pieces of colored tile, presumably from the palace roof. We could see the outlines of old buildings under the earth. It should be a paradise for trained excavators but nothing was being done. The Mongolians have little knowledge of or interest in their history, and they are suspicious of outsiders.

With so little left, it was hard to realize that from there, most of the then civilized world was conquered and ruled.

First Genghis Khan conquered China, and then turned westward. Each Mongolian horseman rode one horse and led three fresh mounts. In this way, his armies easily covered fifty miles a day. As he conquered country after country, he recruited more warriors. He broke up his armies into ten thousand horsemen each, and stationed them strategically across Asia and Europe. With each army were Chinese engineers to build catapults and other siege weapons to use in overwhelming walled cities. Relays of messengers like the "Pony Express" carried his orders and brought back information.

One of his armies had reached Moscow and another was besieging Vienna, when Genghis Khan died.

It was important that his death be kept secret from the world until his four sons could be notified and return to Karakorum. As a result, every human being who was so unfortunate as to see the funeral cortege of the Great Khan's body being returned to Karakorum was murdered. His burial place is still unknown.

Under Mongolian custom at the time, no fighting should take place until two years after the death of the Khan. As a result, the siege of Vienna was lifted. If Genghis Khan had not died when he did his mounted hordes might have swept as far as the English Channel. This is as far as Hitler got. And he didn't start from far-off Mongolia.

One of the purposes of Phil Crowe's visit to Outer Mongolia was to learn what he could about the descendants of the Great Khan's horses. There were reported to be two herds of them still roaming wild in the country but we never saw any.

That night at the spa there was an entertainment followed by a dance. It was up to one of our group to perform. We nominated John Hanes, who has a beautiful voice. He sang "Swing Low Sweet Chariot" and "The Battle Hymn of the Republic." His audience couldn't understand a word but obviously were captivated by the rhythm.

After the show the girls and women sat along one wall in straight-backed chairs. The men sat opposite them. It was like dancing school except for the dances. And the floor was worse than a second-rate barn.

I spotted a pretty Mongolian girl seated across the hall. I went over, bowed low and gestured that I would like to dance with her. When she climbed down from her chair she turned out to be only four feet tall to my six feet one. With rubber-soled shoes, rough floor, strange music and a girl who hardly came to my waist, it was tough going. It soon turned out, as far as our feet were concerned, there was a definite conflict of interest. We ended up doing a sort of Mongolian mazurka.

In order to get a girl as tall as my shoulder, I had to settle for two hundred pounds on the hoof.

The next morning we were to fly back to Ulan Bator at 9:00 A.M. from a nearby pasture "airfield." The plane arrived an hour late but "Dumbo" said there would be another delay as the pilots were hungry and had decided to eat. We could see they had his sympathy.

In the spa hotel there was an oversized pool table so we decided to have a game while we waited. All fifteen balls, plus the cue ball, were appropriately colored a solid bright red. There were small, almost indistinguishable numbers from 1 to 15 in black. The Mongolians pay no attention to these nor do they necessarily use the unnumbered ball as the cue ball. They just use the ball that will give them the easiest shot.

The cues were so crooked it looked as though they had been hammered out of sickles. There was no chalk, so we used aspirin tablets.

When eleven o'clock passed, we were afraid that though the pilots had been fed, "Dumbo" might get hungry. We took off at 11:15 A.M. and arrived at Ulan Bator at twelve-thirty. It was a smooth flight and though we took the precaution of sitting up front, it wasn't necessary. The bucket wasn't called into play.

The next day, Friday, May 14, 1965, we visited the only practicing lamasary in Ulan Bator. The Communists have practically done away with religion in Outer Mongolia. There are only about a hundred older monks and few young men are entering the priesthood. Not so long ago, nearly eighty per cent of the men were Buddhist priests and presumably celibate. This custom and venereal disease accounted for the dwindling population. Since VD has been largely eradicated and the men have taken up more normal lives, the birth rate has gone up. Half of the million people in Outer Mongolia are eighteen or younger.

Outside the temple there were half a dozen platforms about two by six feet. The end away from the temple was about eighteen inches off the ground, and the other end about two feet. A worshiper would put a dirty rag at the low end. Backing off a few feet, he would run at the platform, place his hands on the rag, and slide forward the length of the platform. He would repeat this performance over and over again. The rag was evidently to prevent splinters.

Inside several dozen shaven-headed priests in golden (not saffron) robes were chanting in unison. In the background were scores of butter lights—wicks floating in butter—often rancid. These were supposedly lit by the worshipers. Since we didn't see any—except the gymnasts outside—we suspected that the monks had provided their own illumination.

After the ceremony, the head lama invited us into his ger. He was an impressive, fine-looking, friendly man. He sat cross-legged facing the entrance with low seats for us on either side of him. On his left was the usual terrifying mound of "goodies" which were one of the hazards of ger-visiting. We had seen them in the lowliest gers.

While we were drinking our buttered tea, I saw out of the corner of my eye a lama concocting for us some devil's brew. I thought I saw the eye of a newt.

After our drinking of this potion we were shown the

library of the lamasary. It contained many beautiful old manuscripts and scrolls but we were told that there was not a history book on the United States or Europe in the whole collection.

The last evening we were given a farewell dinner by Intourist. The head of the office was there, "Dumbo" and others. It was a gay dinner with wine and much too much vodka—and the inevitable mutton.

I gagged down two slices of the latter while drinking toasts, individually, with our Mongolian friends. They were eating mutton like peanuts.

We got up from the table.

I fell flat on my face.

20

A Ghetto with Wings

IT WAS almost like returning home to get back to the Siberia Hotel in Irkutsk. Not only were the accommodations familiar but we did not have to subsist on mutton. For the first time in two weeks we had vegetables and fruit juices.

We were reluctant to leave Irkutsk but were looking forward to seeing Russia out of the windows of our compartment on the Trans-Siberian railroad. In five days and four nights to Moscow, we could learn a lot about the country—the houses, the roads, the prosperity of the people, the degree of electrification, etc.

We knew it would not be a very comfortable trip and we had been warned that the food would be poor and scarce. We stocked up on chocolate bars, canned mandarin oranges, tomato juice and vodka. Mary and I even had sleeping bags bought in Japan on the advice of a friend who had taken the

Trans-Siberian railroad and for a long time had insect bites to prove it.

The six of us had three staterooms from Irkutsk to Moscow confirmed months in advance. When we learned in Irkutsk that there were only two staterooms on the train coming through from Peking, the Crowes made arrangements to fly instead. They had been traveling for several months and were anxious to get home. Then John got sick and the Haneses decided to fly also.

Mary and I were at the railroad station at 6:30 A.M. for the 8:00 A.M. train. When it arrived, we were told that some Red Chinese who had come from Peking had locked themselves in the compartments and would not leave.

We returned to our hotel and were fortunate in securing air passage that night at 11:00 P.M. for Moscow. Not only were we fortunate in getting a reservation, but we were even more fortunate in getting our ticket issued. Apparently there was only one person in Irkutsk who could make out the tickets. Since it was Sunday, she was not at her office. It took six hours to track her down and get the proper tickets even though we had secured reservations.

It was the worst flight we have ever taken. The international Russian planes are quite good because they have to compete with those in other countries. The one from Khabarovsk to Irkutsk was fair. The plane from Irkutsk to Moscow was abominable. It was large, hot and closely packed with unwashed humans. The plane was not pressurized but the temperature was regulated by someone up front (not up there). We, as individuals, were not able to regulate our own temperature by turning an overhead valve as we were accustomed to doing.

Russia is run on the theory "Papa knows best." The "Papa" in our plane must have had his instructions from a higher-ranking bureaucrat. He followed them meticulously. He would turn on the heat for half an hour, then turn it off and blast the cabin with freezing air for another thirty minutes. Then back to the heat.

We and our fellow passengers alternately shed and donned our clothing. The lights were so dim it was impossible to read. At first we thought the midnight snack would be a welcome diversion. That was before we saw the galley. Its peeling paint and general filth cured us of that idea. The lone lavatory and toilet might just as well have been an outhouse, except it did not have even a mail order catalogue.

We realized the Russians had scored another first in space—the first flying ghetto.

We had been advised to stay at the National Hotel in Moscow but we did not know where we would be. There is an old saying, "You pay your money and you take your choice." In Russia you pay your money and go where they send you. For your dollars in advance all you receive are coupons entitling you to a room—name of hotel and price of room unspecified.

Fortunately we found ourselves at the National. The bedrooms were large with high ceilings and turn-of-the-century furniture. Our two beds were in an enormous alcove that could be separated from the rest of the room by drawing two heavy red velvet curtains.

Except for the numerous mirrors and chandeliers, everything in our room was red or gold. We loved it, but it would have given Conrad Hilton nightmares.

Our first day in Moscow we, like all tourists, went to visit Lenin's tomb. We chose a bad day. It was the first day of school summer vacation and thousands of children were in line to view Comrade Lenin or a reasonable facsimile thereof. They were nice-looking, clean, well-dressed kids.

We were in line for more than an hour as the children filed by. They appeared to be not just a new generation but a different race. They did not have the familiar dull, stupid, cloddish peasant look of their elders—including their country's leaders.

The general unattractiveness of the middle-aged Russian is usually attributed to the fact that "the cream of the crop," the intellectuals and aristocracy, were liquidated during the revolution. Then who spawned these nice-looking kids?

Finally, our line's turn came and we shuffled slowly into the tomb and past the open coffin. How much was Lenin and how much was wax only Madame Tussaud would be able to tell. We recalled the joke we had heard some years ago. Ivan when asked how he is replies, "I'm as well off as Lenin. They won't feed me and they won't bury me."

We contrasted this vulgar display with the dignity and solemnity of the occasion when we paid a last visit to Winston Churchill at his catafalque the night before his funeral.

The next day we had luncheon with our ambassador and Mrs. Foy Kohler. We had known them before and crossed on the S.S. *United States* with them when he was taking up his post in Moscow. It was fun being with gay and knowledgeable people and having our first really good meal in a month or more.

Our ambassador explained that he had had to walk out of eight diplomatic receptions in the recent past. Instead of attacking the United States straightforwardly in a way that could be answered, the Russians and their stooges followed Khrushchev's childish bad manners and made insulting toasts —without, happily, pounding their shoes on the table.

A few years before I had picketed the Russian residence in New York City at the time of the Hungarian revolution. We had been at a friend's cocktail party and saw several thousand people protesting in front of Khrushchev's home, where a reception was being given. Only the Russians and their stooges were attending.

Mary and I were going to the theater and to a private dance afterward so I was dressed in a tuxedo. I gave my ticket to Charlie and changed into old clothes before joining the picket line.

There were dozens of police who insisted that we "keep moving." Roughly four abreast, we would file back and forth before the Russian Embassy. Every time guests would arrive or depart, we would shake our fists and shout "Murderers!"

I trudged back and forth for about an hour. Our ranks dwindled to about a hundred and most of the guests had left. Then four men came out and got into a taxi. I rushed forward, shook my fist and exclaimed, "Murderers!"

A cop tapped me on the shoulder. "Those are four American bartenders going home."

Our best evening in Moscow was when we were invited to the Austrian Embassy for a concert given by the famous Salzburg Mozart group, followed by a delicious supper. Ambassador Wodak and his wife were old friends of ours.

Since the party was in the suburbs, we had hired a car for the evening. As we left, we were both conscious of a Russian soldier guard eyeing us suspiciously. He followed us in a commandeered private car and stopped us on a lonely stretch of road. After ten minutes of conversation with our driver, we proceeded on our way and the soldier turned back. We gathered it was a case of mistaken identity.

It reminded us of the time I was taken for King Leopold of Belgium in Cartagena, Colombia, in 1952. While visiting a cathedral there, a woman spoke to our guide in Spanish. When we emerged from the church there was a small crowd awaiting us. Our guide whispered that when the woman asked if I were King Leopold, who was expected that day, he had answered "yes."

Apparently she had spread the word. When we arrived at a war memorial a few blocks away, several hundred people had gathered. We inspected the monument and returned to our car. If the crowd was disappointed that I had not deposited the usual floral tribute they did not show it.

We then motored to the old fort on the outskirts of the

city where we were treated as ordinary tourists. Just as we
were leaving the King arrived with a military escort.

At luncheon at the Yacht Club that day, we heard over the
radio that the police were looking for a man who had been
masquerading as the King.

The culprit was never apprehended.

On Wednesday we flew to Leningrad with the intention
of spending two days in the Hermitage. We were surprised
and disappointed to learn that the Hermitage would be
closed on Thursday so we had only half of Wednesday there.
When we could not get into the Hermitage on Thursday,
we motored out into the countryside to see an old palace of
the czars, now called "Pushkin" Village. Though it had
been heavily bombed in the war, it had been beautifully
reconstructed and most of the furniture and art had been
saved.

The Intourist office in Leningrad said Moscow Intourist
never knows that the Hermitage is *always* closed on Thurs-
days, and has been for many years. We politely pointed out
this fact to Intourist in Moscow on our return so that other
tourists would not be similarly disappointed. (We could
have gone any day in the week.) The Intourist officials could
not have cared less and made no notes of the Thursday
closing.

Moscow is a strange city that is somehow depressing. The
streets are eight and ten lanes wide, where two lanes would
have been more than adequate for the meager traffic—mostly
trucks. The architecture is abominable. The university and
four other buildings of which the Russians are very proud
are very similar. We decided they were built from the
rejected blueprints of the Woolworth Building. Their new
workers' apartments make our slum clearance housing look
decent.

Mary and I had two evenings alone in Moscow after the
others left. The one that should have been fun was dull. The
one we thought would be quiet, was gay.

We made reservations at what we were assured was the best night spot in town. It was a three-story house that had obviously been built before the revolution. The wide marble staircases were covered with threadbare red carpeting. As we ascended them we could see private parties in the large, high-ceilinged rooms on each floor.

Our restaurant was on the third floor. In the middle of what had become the dance floor was a large marble fountain with a number of overweight nymphs. I can best describe it by saying it seemed to be all bosoms and buttocks. The sculptor must have been an admirer of Peter Paul Rubens.

We had a good table for two and at our left was what appeared to be a pre-wedding party of about twenty. Vodka was flowing like vodka. Everyone got drunk but no one got happy. Two of the men stumbled into the pool at the bottom of the fountain while trying to dance to the three-piece orchestra. We decided the pianist, drummer and violinist had maybe been introduced to each other but had never played together before.

Our last night we planned on a routine dinner at our hotel. It turned out to be a gay evening. As hotel residents, we had a good table on the tiny dance floor. When we saw people trying to get in, we had our table progressively enlarged until we had three Russian couples sitting with us. Several of them spoke English and translated for the others. We all danced and laughed together until quite late—for Moscow.

We were not sorry to leave Russia. The sights had been interesting and the people friendly. Somehow, perhaps from preconceived ideas, we sensed an underlying oppression.

Having heard so much about the relaxed Soviet attitude, I naively thought that I would be able to buy a Western newspaper in Moscow—even though it might be a few days old. When I voiced my surprise at not being able to do so to our guide she replied, "You know why."

Part Five

21

The Bridge of No Return

THE STATE Department asked Mary to take a trip around the world in 1966. The objective was for her to talk with her many friends and point out to them that much could be done in the various countries by volunteers. So many of the developing countries seemed to think that progress came only through government.

For the first time her way was paid by the State Department. Since I had retired from Galey and Lord January 1, 1964, I accompanied her, naturally financing my part of the trip.

When we flew into Korea in January, most of our fellow passengers were soldiers replacing those stationed in Korea, who had volunteered for duty in Vietnam.

We did not know what to expect of Seoul, and it was just as we subconsciously expected—a nondescript, sprawling and shapeless city. Most of the buildings in the area of our hotel were four to six stories high, built of brick or concrete many years ago. There was quite a lot of construction going on, but some of it did not look too substantial. Work on one seven-story building had been stopped as it had started to lean.

Our hotel, the Chosun, was clean but old-fashioned. It was built of heavy masonry. A year later, when we were in Punta del Este, Uruguay, we agreed that the San Raphael there reminded us of the Chosun.

There were no chairs in the lobby, evidently because they wished to discourage loiterers. This lack was more than compensated for by a waitress in the bar who was so pretty she made drinking a pleasure.

Cooking in Korea is done over *yontans*. These are a sort of "briquet" made of low-grade anthracite, which is plentiful there. They are about ten inches in diameter and six to eight inches high and perforated from top to bottom with a number of holes about one-half inch in diameter. *Yon* means locust and *tan* coal. When you cut a locust stalk it has many holes. Hence, "locust coal."

Yontans are hard to ignite, like charcoal, but burn for hours. Two of them will suffice for the average house for twenty-four hours. They cost about four cents apiece.

There are no chimneys over the *yontans*. Instead, the almost smokeless heat they give off is led under the floor to the other side of the room, warming it nicely. The Koreans have been using radiant heat for centuries. I found the floor very comfortable to my stockinged feet when I sat on a cushion on the floor at luncheon in one of the best restaurants. I was guest of a Korean friend at a small men's luncheon while Mary was off with some women. We had all kinds of strange and exotic dishes including "Kimchi," the most popular native dish, which is strangely enough affecting the architecture of the country.

Kimchi is made of cabbage and is something like sauerkraut. They eat it at every meal. Heavily seasoned cabbage is put in jars two and a half feet high and buried in the ground for anywhere from four or five days to several months, depending upon the time of the year. They leave it to ferment a little. "Rot" would be a better word as actually there is little fermentation.

They have not been able to build apartment buildings in Korea because only those on the ground floor could prepare the Kimchi; apparently it is not available in the stores. In Korea, you don't "roll your own," you rot it.

Our visit to the silk market was worth it, despite the fact that it was the worst fire trap we have ever seen. Beautiful silks and brocades were displayed in hundreds of small stalls lining the myriad narrow aisles. These ran in all directions without any apparent floor plan. The market was like a huge rabbit warren.

There were very few windows but the whole place was brilliantly lighted by hundreds of large naked light bulbs hanging from the ceiling. The latter was cobwebbed with miles of extension cords. Each stall seemed to be plugged into a neighbor's lighting system. I wondered how they ever figured out who owed what light bill.

We never saw even one pail of water in the building for fire protection.

Seoul is growing so fast—now three and a half million—that they have a transportation problem even worse than New York's. There are numerous trolley cars and two kinds of buses—the usual large ones and small ones little larger than Volkswagen station wagons. Women are employed to jam people into the buses. The women are so rough that just before we got there the government started a sort of "charm school" to teach them better manners. It is hard to be charming while pushing someone into a bus with one foot.

It was cold in January in Korea, with the temperature varying between 15 and 25 degrees Fahrenheit. Many of the pedestrians wore white cotton masks over their mouths and noses—like operating room nurses. This was for protection against cold, not germs as in Japan.

Family feeling is strong and the birth of a child is a great occasion. Every child is considered one year old at birth and his next birthday is New Year's Day. If he is born on December 31, he is two years old on January 1 by Korean standards—one day old by ours.

Most marriages are arranged and love marriages are rare. The parents' consent is required by law up to the age of thirty.

Korea has one of the highest literacy rates in the world. As a result, their people are educated and efficient. Since they have few raw materials, their economic future lies in importing them and then processing them.into finished goods for export. Their standard of living, though low as we would measure it, is one of the highest in Asia. They boast that "in five years we'll be where Taiwan is today."

They have never forgotten what the United States has done to protect them and give them a decent chance to better themselves. They have sent their soldiers to give the South Vietnamese the same opportunity.

Our last day in Korea was the best. We motored an hour and a half to Panmunjom and the Demilitarized Zone (DMZ) thirty miles to the north. We left at eight o'clock and the soft morning light and long shadows softened the harshness of the rather squalid houses on the outskirts of Seoul. They are so close together that, seen from a little distance, those on the steep hills seem to have been built on top of each other. The countryside was a light tan in color and almost devoid of trees. The Japanese had cut down most of them for lumber between 1910 and 1945, during their occupation. There were hundreds of dry rice paddies on the flat plains on both sides of the road. The ridges between them turned the countryside into a gigantic waffle. We saw very few animals. Since only twenty-one per cent of Korea is arable, they cannot afford the luxury of grazing lands.

The road running north was hard-paved and two lanes wide. There was very little traffic. To our left was a railroad. It ended at the last town south of the DMZ. From there north, the tracks had been torn up. When we motored through a small village and saw a sign, "Number One store of Miss Yong and Miss Sue," we knew we were getting near the border and our troops. "Number One" means "the best" in Korea. If anything is terrible, our G.I.s refer to it as "Number Ten."

We passed a few troop carriers and half a dozen tanks. Occasionally we saw a group of green quonset huts surrounded by a single fence of barbed wire with elevated watchtowers at intervals—a soldier with a machine gun in each one. As we got nearer the border, there were two fences of barbed wire ten feet apart with rolls of barbed wire between, and the watchtowers were closer together. We were reminded that 55,000 forgotten American servicemen were on guard in Korea. Not more than fifteen per cent were ever on leave at one time.

We passed a very big base on the right. There was a banner over the closely guarded entrance, "Gateway to the Defenders of Freedom's Frontier." A few miles farther on at another base, there was a sign, "Sleep soundly tonight, the Seventh Cavalry is awake." As we approached the border there was a crude painting of a G.I. with an arrow through his head. Caption: "Be careful, Indian territory."

Our road ended at a river. The bridge had been destroyed during the war and never rebuilt. A short by-pass had been built to the abandoned railroad embankment to our left. From there, a new steel bridge had been constructed on the old railroad pillars, which were in better condition than those on the old roadway. We had to wait there as the new bridge was only one lane wide. It was very long and M.P.s

directed traffic by shortwave radio. We were told four
vehicles were coming our way. When two jeeps and two
troop carriers had passed we were given the "Go Ahead"
signal.

Meanwhile, we had been carefully checked. It reminded
us of going through "Checkpoint Charlie" in the Berlin
Wall a few years earlier.

We swung left toward the railroad embankment and
then right over the very long bridge. Ahead and above us
was a sign, "Freedom Bridge." Behind us was a very large
tank with its gun and searchlight trained straight down the
bridge. In the turret, very much on the alert, were two
Americans, one black and one white. After we had crossed
the bridge we saw signs, "mined," on either side of the road.
It seems the mines had been left over from the war. Since
they had been planted by both sides, no one knew just where
they were. Except for one G.I. who had gone hunting ten
days before and had his foot blown off.

After several more inspections of our papers we arrived
at the U.S. headquarters in the DMZ. There were several
quonset huts and an officers lounge with a sign over the door,
"The Monastery." It was tastefully furnished with a cheerful fire in the huge fireplace.

We gathered from the few officers we talked to that they
knew they were "expendable" and would be wiped out
quickly if the North Koreans violated the armistice.

In the distance, as far as you could see, was a barren
countryside. Close at hand was as fine a group of "spit and
polish" soldiers as you could find anywhere in the world.
This outpost of the United States could have been Bucking-
ham Palace. The men must have been especially selected.
None of them was under six feet and most of them were
taller. They carried themselves like West Pointers. Their
shoes and buttons glistened, their white belts and helmets
were immaculate.

We appreciated all this more a half hour later when we compared them with their Red counterparts, North Koreans and Chinese. The latter wore long shapeless coats of a shoddy brown material with Red insignia. In spite of the cold—about twenty-five degrees—our men didn't wear their long overcoats. The Red soldiers slouched, ours stood erect.

The DMZ is 400 meters wide and winds 151 miles across the Korean Peninsula. Down the middle runs the Military Demarcation Line. It does not follow the original line of the 38th Parallel. The eastern part is north of the parallel and the western part dips a little to the south of it. It was the line of battle when the fighting stopped.

The Demarcation Line is marked by 1,292 yellow markers spaced irregularly, like out-of-bounds markers on a golf course. The markers are printed in Korean and English on the side facing south, and in Korean and Chinese on the north.

Each side is allowed one thousand men in its half of the zone. Three hundred Americans and seven hundred Koreans patrol the southern half. The Turks and Thais still had troops in South Korea but not in the DMZ. North Korea and Red China are still at war with the United Nations, as no peace treaty has ever been negotiated.

About seventy-five yards south of the Demarcation Line the Koreans have built a small, beautiful building, half shrine and half museum, as a memorial to the men of fifteen nations who fought under the UN banner.

The Neutral Nations Supervisory Commission meets at least once a week in accordance with the provisions of the armistice. The Czech and Polish representatives live to the north of the line, and the Swedish and Swiss to the south of it.

Besides the meetings of the Neutral Commission, there are frequent confrontations between the two sides that had been involved in the fighting.

The buildings where these meetings are held are in a "Joint Security Area." Seven long, low buildings stand parallel to each other straddling the Military Demarcation Line. A strip of yellow paint divides each building in half and even the conference tables. The houses maintained by our side are painted blue and the Reds' are painted green.

We were lucky in that a meeting was being held when we were there. Either side can call a meeting whenever it wishes. It is usually the Reds who do so. Meetings are always held at 11 A.M. sharp. The side calling the meeting starts talking. Only one man speaks for each team and all speeches are translated by interpreters.

We watched through the windows. The men on our side of the yellow line down the middle of the table were obviously soldiers. This did not seem to be true of the Reds. One of their advisers was dressed in a military uniform but wearing plaid Argyle socks. He was probably a political commissar. We could not tell the rank of the Reds because they had abolished all outward evidence of it.

A Colonel Charlton headed the United Nations delegation. On his right was a Korean officer, on his left was an American colonel. The Reds immediately objected to the latter's presence, saying it was against the commission's rules. When Colonel Charlton asked them to point out the rule they were unable to do so, but still objected.

All proceedings were broadcast outside over a loudspeaker. We never knew why, as there were only a few dozen soldiers of both sides and ourselves within earshot. When we left they were still arguing the point of whether or not the American colonel had a right to be there. We never did find out why the meeting was called. At one point Colonel Charlton asked them if they "had come to play games or did they have something to discuss?"

It was a typical example of trying to negotiate with the Communists. We recalled that the United States alone had suffered sixty-two thousand casualties after the "peace talks" began in Korea.

Part of the armistice agreement was that neither side should build up its forces beyond the status quo which existed when the agreement was signed.

In order to bypass the agreed ports of entry, and avoid inspection by the Neutral Nations Inspection Teams, a completely new railroad was built between Manchuria and North Korea. Probably some of the freight cars on those tracks are those stolen from South Korea after World War II.

After the close of that war a conference to explore means of uniting the Korean nation was held in the Duksu Palace in Seoul. A UN team met daily for nearly six months with a Communist one headed by General Shtykoff of the Soviet Union and members from North Korea and Red China participating. The Communists would not agree to UN-supervised elections in North Korea. In fact, only one point of agreement was reached. Because the South is the breadbasket of the peninsula, it was agreed that the South would send grain to the North and the North, in turn, would provide electric power to the South.

Two trainloads of grain were loaded into scarce rolling stock and sent north. As soon as these trains crossed the 38th Parallel the Communists incarcerated the crews, kept not only the grain but the cars and engines as well. They then pulled the switches so the South lived by candlelight until army barges were brought to Uchon and Pusan harbors, giving rationed electricity. Not until power plants could be built in the South was normal service restored.

At the time of the armistice after the Korean War, the Communists had no air force in North Korea. When we were there in January 1966, the best intelligence credited them with having five hundred planes, mostly jets. The United Nations made a tape recording of an official North Korean radio broadcast by the chief of their General Staff in which he said, "The North Korean combat capabilities have been strengthened in a proportion incomparable to the time of the ending of the war." When this tape was replayed before the armistice commission, the Reds denied their violations. The fortifications they have built in the DMZ, contrary to the armistice terms, can be clearly seen.

In spite of the Reds' unbroken record of never living up to their agreements whether it be in Berlin, Korea or Vietnam, the United Nations scrupulously observed the rules for four years. Finally on June 21, 1957, the United Nations Command said the provisions were suspended until the Communists agreed to comply with them.

Before leaving the "Joint Security Area," Mary and I ascended a little hill. From there we could see the only bridge over the river marking the Demarcation Line. It is known as "The Bridge of No Return."

On the way back to Seoul we observed troops on maneuvers. Most of the tanks, troop carriers and jeeps confined themselves to the main roads. Occasionally we saw huge tanks squeezing between little huts, with the muzzles of their guns showing above the thatched roofs.

We passed a number of hillsides covered with small mounds of earth. These were burial grounds and each mound covered a body. They were unmarked because after the funeral procession the mourners never return to the grave. Instead, the "spirit tablet" is returned to the house and food offerings placed before it twice a day. Special food is prepared on the first and fifteenth of every month. Members of the family wail before the "spirit tablet" for fifteen minutes and then eat the food. Mothers are mourned for one year and fathers for three.

The next morning, as we took off for Hong Kong on the superb Cathay Pacific Airline, we looked forward to being in Vietnam again in a few days. I recalled the sign we had seen. "Sleep soundly tonight, the Seventh Cavalry is awake."

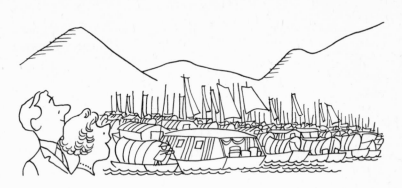

22

The Most Vibrant
City in the World

HONG KONG has changed a lot since I was there the first time in 1927 but it is still one of the most exciting places on earth. At night the "Constellation of Hong Kong" now has ten times as many lights as forty years ago but its shape is still the same.

Seen after dark and from Kowloon on the mainland, the island of Hong Kong looks as though the Milky Way, the Big Dipper, Orion, etc., had all been merged into one. The lights twinkle from the water's edge to the Peak 1,800 feet above. Then they are less numerous where man leaves off and God takes over.

On the opposite side of the island of Hong Kong from the city of Victoria is Repulse Bay. I swam there on my first visit. It turned out to be inappropriately named. It was here that the Japanese made their first landing on the island in World War II.

The most interesting thing to see while in Hong Kong is missed by most forty-eight hour tourists shopping for bargains. I never heard of it on my first trip but did see it in 1955 in spite of my malaria. We visited it again in 1966. I refer to Aberdeen, which is a floating village. There thousands of people live on sampans from birth to death. They eat, sleep and procreate in this floating ghetto. There was no way of telling how many people existed on each sampan. The fascinating, grubby, friendly children were always in the majority.

The sampans were so close together that they almost hid what would be the world's largest open sewer if it were not for the tides. Nevertheless children splashed in the small occasional open spaces.

There is a narrow channel between the sampan-congested banks. Large junks slipped in and out. Some were festooned with drying fish nets, others were loaded with all varieties of cargo. On board were both sexes of all ages. These were floating homes too.

At the end of the estuary the people lived in tumble-down shacks, built on stilts, with rickety boardwalks at intervals. There was nothing but mud below. Presumably the tide covers this a few hours a day or the stench would be worse.

There were fires burning in nearly every shack and sampan. Why the whole place has not gone up in a flaming holocaust is a mystery.

Hong Kong must be the most vibrant city in the world. You can sense its throbbing but its pulse is uneven. In the business section the scores of modern skyscrapers and the hurrying men in dark business suits remind you of Wall Street. Three blocks back from the waterfront on Queen's Road is another world. The stores are smaller and rather cluttered. The signs and street banners are decorated with strange and fascinating symbols unintelligible to us but the ABC's of hundreds of millions of fellow human beings.

Lacing the two sections together are the double-decker

buses and the double-decker trolleys. Off Queen's Road leading up the hill are narrow streets crawling with people jostling each other between piles of wonderful-looking fresh vegetables and fruits.

On the crest of the hill, there are large and expensive houses and apartments. A funicular runs to the Peak. The view from the top is unique. Without taking a step, you can see three worlds.

Below you on the few acres of flat ground are the tall white office buildings. Climbing the hill between them and you are the almost equally high apartment houses. Only two open spaces are to be seen. One is the Hong Kong Club with its lawn and tennis courts. The other is the race track. If the time ever comes when you cannot see both of these with the naked eye, then you will not be able to find the Union Jack with binoculars.

If you turn around and look south there are half a dozen beautiful bays dotted with islands. But surprisingly this side of the Peak has retained much of its greenery. There are many beautiful houses nestled among tall trees and flowering shrubs.

Mary and I savored this slightly familiar sight, then gazed across at Kowloon on the mainland. We had spent a full day there and seen the new housing erected for the tens of thousands of Chinese refugees from Red China. They were not quartered in tents or makeshift huts but in substantial apartment buildings five to eight stories high, covering many square blocks of the sprawling ever-growing city. Many of the buildings had schools or play areas on their roofs.

Beyond Kowloon we could see the open country extending to the nearby Chinese border. This was where Winston's brave little Chinese sister-in-law, San San, who had risked everything to escape from Red China, met for the first time her real mother, whose existence she had not known of a year earlier.

23

A Lump in the Throat Versus a Tear in the Eye

OUR PLANE from Hong Kong was almost deserted. There were only a couple of dozen passengers. With so many airliners flying all over that part of the world, apparently most people preferred a plane that didn't stop in Saigon unless that was their destination.

Our approach was not the usual long, gliding slide into the airport to which we had become accustomed. Instead, we came in high and spiraled down in tight circles over the city. Apparently the pilot didn't want to take any chances of being shot at over the countryside.

We were delayed nearly a half an hour because of air traffic, and flew in small circles. I didn't know there were so many different kinds of military aircraft; all apparently designed for some specific purpose. The airport was so crowded that the smaller planes often took off two abreast.

I was particularly interested in the large helicopters jockeying on the runways with their gunners' heads sticking out of their turrets until just before takeoff. Apparently there is no air conditioning in helicopters. Probably part of McNamara's economy program.

We were met by Bob Barr of our Embassy who fortunately lost his way into the city. This prolonged our fascinating trip to our hotel. We could see many changes since our previous visit. The jinrikshas had been replaced with pedicabs. Many of the bicycles had been superseded by motorbikes, motorcycles and scooters. A disappointing number of Vietnamese had adopted Western dress, but they were in the minority.

Saigon is noteworthy for its trees. You have to give the French credit. They planted trees—though they did little to develop the human resources of Indochina.

I was glad to see that my memory had not been playing tricks for eleven years. The girls in their Au Dais were just as petite and lovely as I remembered them. They looked like dolls and I guess a good many of them *were* playthings.

Our baggage was unloaded quickly at the Hotel Caravelle and Bob Barr immediately parked the car about a block away. Ever since the hotel was bombed a few months before no cars were allowed to stand in front of the hotel any longer than was necessary to unload. At nighttime we had to leave our car a block away and walk through the barricade.

The Continental Hotel across the square had never been bombed. It had a dining room open to the street and a large sidewalk café. Half a block away was another restaurant and bar surrounded by barbed wire and sand bags. We were told that those who paid tribute to the Viet Cong did not need to take precautions against bombings. We decided that we preferred the open ones to those with the inadequate defenses. The bar we liked the most was in our hotel—on the eighth floor!

We did not have time to unpack before rushing to a reception given by Ambassador Cabot Lodge for Vice President Humphrey and Averell Harriman. The Vice President was as surprised to see his fellow Minnesotan as Ambassador Harriman was to see his brother-in-law's brother.

The Viet Cong (the successors to the Viet Minh of the war against the French) could have hit the jackpot that night. Besides Humphrey, Lodge and Harriman, General Westmoreland and other leaders were included among the guests for cocktails and the delicious buffet supper. We were glad to dine on good American food even though we had learned to tolerate seaweed and fried maggots in our travels.

What made the occasion so special was that for the first time in months many of the wives were present. Most of them had been evacuated to Bangkok months before and were in Saigon for only a few days. Emily Lodge and I reminisced about our times at the UN when Cabot was head of the delegation and Mary was a member.

Security was particularly strict that evening. Besides showing our credentials several times, mirrors on long poles were passed under arriving cars to make sure that no bombs had been suspended underneath.

During the evening I watched TV movies of the Honolulu Conference in the library. The Vice President entered the room just in time to see himself descending, smiling, from a plane a few days before.

TV was new in Saigon when we were there and this was the first week it had been shown. Because there were no adequate facilities, it was being beamed from a U.S. airplane overhead. The programs lasted three hours each evening. Two hours were broadcast in Vietnamese and one hour in English.

TV was introduced partly as entertainment for our soldiers and partly as a low-keyed propaganda medium aimed at the Vietnamese—one with which the Viet Cong could not compete. Since there were few privately owned TV sets in Vietnam, they were set up in parks, squares and shop windows. The crowds that gathered to watch them were inviting targets for Viet Cong bombs.

We found it hard to reconcile the idea that the Viet Cong really represented the peasants in the villages and the fact that in the last two years the VC had murdered (and usually tortured) more than four thousand village leaders selected by the villagers; never had so many people been killed by their friends!

Apparently there was some artillery fire and bombing outside Saigon the first night we were there. We heard and saw none of it though some others in the hotel went to the roof to watch.

The first place we visited the next morning turned out to be an orphanage we had seen eleven years before. We immediately recognized it and the woman in charge. She remembered us and seemed pleased we had returned.

The children we had seen had been replaced by another generation, equally appealing.

Saigon did not give the appearance of the capital of a country at war. There were not nearly as many uniformed men in the streets as we expected. Most American servicemen were elsewhere and those who came to the city on leave wore civilian clothes and seemed lonely and pathetic. Naturally, some of them seek out the extremely attractive bar girls—but we also found them devoting their days off to building orphanages or teaching school.

We were surprised when visiting one orphanage to see American servicemen working in the back yard. They were building a dormitory for the kids in their spare time. They had contributed part of their pay to buy some of the material and I suspect they had "scrounged" a lot from the Army. I talked to a lieutenant in an engineer battalion in charge of the volunteer work. He said, "They don't give us enough to do to keep our men busy, and besides, you can't help but love these people."

He was so right. They are like the Nepalese, Tibetans, Mongolians, Burmese, Indonesians and Chinese. They are just as poor and should be as miserable as the Indians. But they have warm hearts and a sense of humor.

The children melt you—particularly in the orphanages. They swarm around you. If you wink an eye or snap your fingers, they dissolve into hysterical laughter. They shout, "O.K.," and if you answer "O.K." they yell "O.K." again. This keeps up until you finally let the echo die out.

You shake their hands a dozen at a time and feel them clawing at your legs. Their big brown eyes crave affection but their lips are smiling. I never decided which was harder —choking back a lump in my throat or blinking a tear from my eye.

One of the most interesting and encouraging things we saw in Saigon was District Eight. The eighth district is the poorest in Saigon—and that's a real superlative when it comes to describing poverty.

Six months earlier about thirty students in the university decided instead of negative protesting they would do something positive and constructive. They began by living in the slums, eating the same slops and not even using a mosquito net at night. When they had won the confidence of the people in district eight, they persuaded them they could do something to better their own lot.

First they got permission to remove the remains from a cemetery to clear a large tract of land. This was enlarged by pumping mud from the river with an old dredge supplied by the government.

We saw women mixing concrete and making and laying concrete blocks. Others were carrying water or sand on both ends of a long pole across their shoulders. All were volunteers of the district building better homes for themselves for the future. The men helped on the project in the evenings after their regular work was done.

Students supervised the work and their leader was a nineteen-year-old boy operating a bulldozer when we met him. He had planned the whole project and had made provision for play areas and parks.

Although actual construction had started less than two months before, two hundred homes would be finished in two more weeks. Then a lottery was to be held and the lucky workers would move into the new homes they had helped to build.

Work was to continue until they had built nearly a thousand small houses—enough for all those who had contributed to the project. There were two problems that could arise. Would the lucky ones continue to work once they had their own homes? Would the people who had taken possession of the half-finished houses get out?

Besides this and other volunteer projects, we saw and heard of many instances where the South Vietnamese government—usually with U.S. aid—was striving to better the lot of its people. Only a pitiful start had been made. The French had done little for them and since their withdrawal the development of the country has been hamstrung by first the Viet Minh and then the Viet Cong—all directed by the Communist leaders of North Vietnam.

We heard many firsthand accounts of how the Viet Cong terrorize the peasants.

We talked with one South Vietnamese woman who was a leader in a little village thirty miles from Saigon. The villagers had been turning over a part of their rice crop to the Viet Cong under threats of terrorism. The Viet Cong kept demanding a larger and larger share. Finally our friend, as the village leader, told her neighbors not to give any more and that she would set the example.

The next day she was supervising the construction of a

small schoolhouse in her village—aided in the work by two American G.I.s on leave. Two men in peasant dress approached with building materials on poles across their shoulders. Suddenly they dropped them, took carbines from under their clothes and shot at the G.I.s, killing one and wounding the other.

That night the Viet Cong came to the village looking for our friend. Fortunately she had gone to Saigon. They tied up her three teachers and threatened to torture them if they did not disclose the leader's whereabouts. After several hours the VC became convinced that the woman they wanted was really in Saigon.

We saw her three days after the incident. She asked us to come to her village as she thought it would be good for morale for American civilians to be seen there. We agreed to go but were denied permission by our authorities.

We learned that forty countries of the free world were helping the South Vietnamese in one way or another. There were several billboards in Saigon listing their names.

Next to that from the United States, the largest contingent of foreign soldiers was from Korea. It had also contributed a complete, fully staffed hospital that Dr. Howard Rusk told Mary was one of the best he had ever seen.

We saw many French among the dedicated men and women of various nationalities, races and religions in Vietnam. Most of them were not fighting in the military sense, but helping just as much and often with just as much risk. We did not meet anyone from Cabot Lodge down who thought that the war could be won for the South Vietnamese on a purely military basis. The average villagers, we were told, were interested (quite naturally) only in security. They were not interested in politics and did not identify themselves with the central government. All they wanted was to be left alone. They were therefore willing to pay for a "little protection" from the Viet Cong. But paying a little blackmail is like being a "little bit pregnant." It never stops there.

All efforts to better the lives of the peasants were being deliberately frustrated by the Viet Cong. If the people were reasonably secure, housed, fed and educated there would be no place for the VC. Ten years before they had held out hope to people who had little to lose. Now the Viet Cong, instead of trying to help the peasants, were determined to see that the South Vietnamese government, with massive American aid, did not help them and win their allegiance.

Our trip to Hue was the most interesting part of our visit to Vietnam. We were delayed forty-five minutes but it was fascinating watching the airport activity. There were truck-loads of South Vietnamese soldiers disappearing solemnly into the large dim holds of cavernous transport planes—like so many Jonahs filing singly into the bellies of flying whales.

On another runway, jet fighter planes were arriving every thirty seconds. Hardly had the yellow braking parachute of one plane popped from its tail like bubble gum, when the next fighter would touch down.

We had been told we would fly in a single engine plane and were relieved when we found a twin-engined Beechcraft. Vietnam is not the best place in the world for a forced landing—and not just because of the rugged terrain.

Our pilot pointed out puffs of black smoke just ahead. They were caused by bomb explosions but we could not see our camouflaged planes below us against the green foliage. Several times we saw small fires started by napalm.

Then we flew over the site of a recent B-52 strike. What destruction—even with conventional bombs. The deep jungle had been ripped apart over an area of many square miles. The brown bomb scars were in vivid contrast to the lush foliage. Some of them seemed to be as large as several football fields. About twenty-five per cent of the area had been stripped of all growth.

I think it is safe to assume that no civilians were hurt in the strike. There were no paddy fields, no openings, no houses for miles around. Only the Viet Cong could have been hiding under that green blanket. They have numerous rest, restraining and storage areas hidden in the jungles. There is no way to destroy them except by the B-52s.

We flew over Chu Lai and Da Nang. There were many ships in both harbors being unloaded by lighters and LSTs. Planes and choppers were landing and taking off from modern airstrips where there were only jungle and marshland a few months before.

Our pilot circled Hue several times so we could get a good look and take pictures. It is sometimes referred to as a miniature Peking. There is an inner walled "forbidden city" where the emperors lived and no one else was allowed. It is surrounded by a moat.

The "forbidden city" is in the center of a much larger area about two miles square. This, too, is surrounded by a water-filled moat and high walls that zigzag like strokes of lightning. The walls are twenty-five feet thick. It was this Citadel that was infiltrated and seized by the Viet Cong during the truce they had proclaimed for the Tet holidays in 1968.

It reminded us from the air of Angkor Wat and the U.S. representative, Al Ball, who met us, later made the same observation.

There is a finished hotel in Hue but since it has never been opened Al invited us to stay with him.

During lunch we heard our first artillery fire on the outskirts of the city. It kept up sporadically the two days and nights we spent in Hue. It seemed trivial, haphazard and unimportant—except to those who died!

In our various briefings we were told that Hue was considered "secure." It was there that the trouble that overthrew the Diem regime started and the students had overthrown several governments since. The North Vietnamese did not want to interfere with the good work being done for the Viet Cong by the students.

Our first night in Hue we went with some friends to an outdoor Chinese restaurant beyond the city limits. The sound of the artillery was much louder. The next morning we realized that we had probably been a little foolish.

On our way home from the restaurant we had passed the police station five blocks from Al Ball's house. Ten minutes later the Viet Cong struck in Hue for the first time. They threw a bomb killing the police chief and wounding seven of his men, five seriously. They escaped in the crowd of civilians who rushed out at the sound of the explosion. The latter would have been endangered if the Viet Cong had been fired upon. If the situation had been reversed, they would have had no such scruples.

In Hue our house (Al Ball's) was on a small side street. There was barbed wire across one end of the street and halfway across the other end. We drove in and out without any trouble so I could not see that the wire was of any use. There was a rifle in our bedroom. Since I have yet to knock over my first shooting-gallery duck, Mary's last line of defense was hardly impregnable.

Everyone we spoke to in Vietnam, regardless of nationality, agreed that the thirty-seven-day bombing truce had probably prolonged the war. Our military adviser to the South Vietnamese Army in Hue told me that before the truce he estimated there were fourteen thousand Viet Cong and North Vietnamese in the surrounding province. Six weeks later there were nineteen thousand. He named a North Vietnamese regiment that had arrived near Hue on December 29. They must have started south on Christmas Eve, when the one-sided truce began.

While in Hue we visited the "forbidden city," which was more impressive from the air than on the ground. Much more enjoyable was a trip late in the afternoon by sampan on the Perfume River. That is its right name and it was not given in jest. We did not smell the "perfume" but we happily did not smell anything at all. Maybe the absence of stench can be considered a perfume. It would be hard to bottle and sell unless it was beautifully packaged and outrageously overpriced.

On our way back from Hue we stopped at our military base in Da Nang to visit a refugee camp. It was the first one we had ever seen in beautiful surroundings. It was situated under tall palm trees edging a beautiful wide sandy beach that ended in a deep blue sea flecked with white.

We went down to the edge of the water to watch the fishermen pulling in their nets and the women sorting over the fish. There were a half dozen American soldiers strolling on the beach. With them was a very beautiful and well-built Vietnamese girl in the briefest bikini I have ever seen. I was glad to see that our boys were spreading Western civilization around the world.

The refugee camp held about a thousand persons. Almost all of them were Montagnards. This seemed to us very significant.

The Montagnards are of a different race from the other Vietnamese, North or South. They are mountain people who have been advocating their own independent country ever since the politicians in Paris pulled the rug out from under the French Army and turned Indochina over to Ho Chi Minh and the Communists.

In the war in Vietnam the Montagnards' traditional attitude was "a plague on both your houses." They had left their villages for the comparative safety of Da Nang not for any love of the Americans but because they had had all they could take from the Viet Cong. As soon as they left their villages they were burned to the ground and the old people left behind murdered by the Liberation Front. They had nothing to go back to.

When we got back to Saigon we found that STIF had called a strike. STIF was nothing like SMERSH. The initials stood for "Saigon Tea Is Fine." Saigon Tea is what the bar girls asked our men to buy for them. It was supposed to be whiskey and water. Instead, it was tea and water and cost 160 piastres (at that time there were 118 piastres to the dollar). The price used to be 80 piastres.

The G.I.s had gone on strike against the high price of Saigon Tea and were passing out STIF pamphlets to all soldiers on leave. They were urged to just sip beer and ignore the girls. The strike did not last long. There were too many, too attractive strike breakers.

Our last day in Saigon we saw the son of a friend of ours who had been very high up in C.I.A. under Allan Dulles. He had just come from interviewing five North Vietnamese defectors. They had infiltrated with their whole unit the preceding April.

They said they had been told that the people of South Vietnam would welcome them with open arms and that theirs would be a triumphal march into Saigon. When they learned the truth they defected but were fiercely proud of what had been accomplished in North Vietnam.

The last thing we saw as we spiraled up from the Saigon airport were the rows of slick jet fighters and bombers lined up in their revetments like thoroughbred race horses in their stalls.

I wondered if history would have been the same if the people of the thirteen colonies had had television pictures every night of the soldiers at Valley Forge.

24

T. I. I.

FROM SAIGON we flew to Kuala Lumpur, Malaysia, and were impressed by the beautiful and imaginative modern architecture there, particularly the new mosque, art museum and university. Near the latter is the Malaysian War Memorial. A semicircular colonnade half surrounds a pool with fountains playing. In the center of the pool is a group of sculptured figures strikingly reminiscent of the statue of the three men raising the flag on the peak of Iwo Jima. The same artist did both.

One day we motored north to Fraser Hill, a former British "hill station." The first part of the trip was through small villages and the latter part through jungle. We were fascinated by the fern trees. Thirty or more feet tall they were exactly like giant ferns. As I peered up at them outlined against the blue sky I understood how Alice must have felt looking up at the toadstool.

It was just north of Fraser Hill in a similar jungle that Jimmy Thompson disappeared a year later. No trace of him has ever been found.

On the way to India from Kuala Lumpur we spent several days in Bangkok. Again Prince and Princess Wan entertained us and we had dinner with Jimmy Thompson, little anticipating it would be the last time we would ever see him.

We were shocked and disappointed to see how things had deteriorated in India. The hope and confidence so evident after independence had given way to disillusionment. India was beginning to strangle on its own bureaucracy. Its only accomplishment (if it can be called that) was the addition of Goa to its territory. Between pious lectures to the world, Nehru had stolen it, prodded by Krishna Menon, his Mephistopheles-like Defense Minister.

(When the Russians brutally put down the Hungarian revolt and the UN Security Council wanted to rebuke them, India, under Nehru, voted with the Soviets. When Russia violated Czechoslovakia in 1968 and the question of censure again came before the Security Council, India, under the leadership of Nehru's daughter, Indira Gandhi, abstained.)

India was even more depressing in 1966 than on our previous visits. In ten years we had seen the mood of the country go from hope to hopelessness and then to something akin to despair. This impression was not gained superficially as a tourist, but from the frank talks we had with our Indian friends. We have many of the latter and they have always been most hospitable to us.

Some suggested that things would not get better until members were elected to their Congress on some qualification other than that they had been in jail under the British. One Indian said, "Things are pretty bad; we are in a mess because we have introduced all kinds of regimentation. No wonder we have trouble raising money in the capital market."

After chronicling for the boys some of the depressing information we picked up, Mary wrote, "Many blame Nehru —with his ideologies—inexpertness—living in the clouds— and his Fabian Marxist training under Laski, which always made him suspicious of and arrogant toward the 'Private Sector.' "

In our travels we have always found it rewarding to read the local classified ads. Here are a few from the Indian papers.

"Wanted—beautiful, healthy, wealthy bride for Punjabi, rich, independent, divorced Brahmin, 28. Rupees, 375 monthly. Future bright, immediate marriage, caste, province immaterial."

"Wanted—smart, beautiful South Indian Brahmin, medical graduate. Bride below 27 years for young and handsome doctor, belonging to a very respectable and well-to-do family. Please reply promptly with full particulars regarding girl and family, enclosing horoscope."

"Wanted—an exceptionally beautiful, smart, tall, slim, good-natured girl (any caste) for a suitable Hindu (Brahmin) youth in service."

"Wanted—Brahmin girls between 25 and 28 to marry my two sons, aged 34 and 31, who are holding high jobs in the government. Girls should be fair, healthy and educated. The undersigned will be coming to India for arrangements on receipt of applications. Horoscope lost and not available."

In Bombay on our last day in India Mary went out into the country with some of the leaders of Planned Parenthood, accompanied by a "mobile van." She was encouraged by the eagerness of the women of all ages for information on birth control. The following day meetings would be held for the men to encourage their cooperation.

She wrote the boys, "After leaving the village last night we were stopped at a railroad crossing and made to stay there until eight trains went by—even though the intervals

between trains were anywhere from five to ten minutes. I
was upset by the delay but my escort calmly said, 'T.I.I.'

" 'What's that?'

" *'This is India.'* "

25

Slight Bows and Dignified Gestures

FROM BOMBAY we flew to Karachi. On our previous trips to Pakistan we found the people very friendly to Americans and grateful for all the help we had given them. But not so in 1966. Our friends had not changed, but the populace had. They blamed the United States for not coming to their aid in the war against India the previous summer.

Pakistan in early 1966 was not a country but a state of mind—a nation with a persecution complex—a people who had lost touch with reality. When I asked one Pakistani general what had the Chinese done that they had suddenly become such great friends, he replied, "The Chinese made several radio broadcasts strongly condemning the Indians." As far as we could ascertain that was the extent of China's aid at that time.

No one who did not travel in Pakistan and India shortly

after their "war" could possibly understand the impact on those two countries. They were both badly scarred and economically set back as a result. The meager resources of both India and Pakistan had been squandered in a suicide pact. It was like two castaways on a raft in the middle of the ocean starting a water fight with their last canteens of fresh water—and over Kashmir, which is of little economic value.

Pakistani Moslems died to bring other Moslems under their flag. The Indians had been indoctrinated to support Nehru's *coup d'état*, which had kept the ancestral home under the Indian flag.

We spent a few days each in Karachi, Lahore and Rawalpindi. In each city we were told that there had been no social contact between Pakistanis and Americans since "the war." All this changed during our visit. In each of the three cities luncheons and dinners were given for us by either our Pakistani or American friends and the guests of each nationality attended. Our U.S. officials were pleased that we had "broken the ice." Mary was even asked to speak over the national radio on "All Pakistan Day," the anniversary of their separation from India.

On our arrival at the Lahore airport we were surprised and touched to be met by an old Pakistani friend, General Shor, his wife and daughter, who had brought flowers for us. The general had rushed from Rawalpindi, where he had just been decorated by President Ayub for his part in the war against India.

The next day our return visit to the Shalamar Gardens was disappointing. The water had been drained from the pools and canals so that they could be freshly painted in honor of Red Chinese dignitaries who were to visit Lahore after Rawalpindi.

In the afternoon it had been arranged for the military to take us to see the Wagah border and villages destroyed by the Indians (after the cease-fire, according to the Pakistanis). Since very few persons had been permitted to go there, several in our consulate were glad of the opportunity to go along.

We saw about what we expected—roofless houses, barren fields and a few pitiful returning villagers searching through the rubble of their homes for anything of value, sentimental or otherwise. Their eyes mirrored the sentiments in their hearts—anger and despair—courage and hate.

We were told by the Pakistanis that the Indians had poisoned the wells before they withdrew to "the original line." Whether or not this was true, we do not know. We never sampled the well water.

Though there were new hotels in Rawalpindi, we stayed at the American Embassy residence. Two of our Pakistani friends had asked us to stay with them but it was thought advisable that we stay "on neutral ground."

The ambassador was not there but in Karachi. The government of Pakistan was being moved from there to the new capital at Islamabad being built outside Rawalpindi. Many of the government departments had not yet been transferred. As a result, Ambassador Walter P. McConaughby split his time between the two cities.

We motored out to see Islamabad and were disappointed. Much had been done since Mary visited the site five years before—including leveling the ground and cutting down any trees. The modern concept of traffic circles at street intersections had been ignored. The architecture was flat, square and unimaginative. The Greek who had been the original planner had been fired but it was too late.

Probably by now the foreign Embassies have been built to lend variety to the architecture, and grass and trees can do a lot.

The road to Islamabad was decorated with flags in honor of the chief of state of the People's Republic of China, Mr. Liu Shao-chi, who would pass that way the next day.

It just happened that we did, too. When we turned out of a side street onto the main road, we found ourselves just behind an army car flying a large green Pakistan flag. It was the first car in the official procession, which was several minutes behind.

We never knew why we were allowed to remain in line unless it was because we were in General Shahid Hamid's chauffeur-driven car with him, on our way to his country place at Muree, thirty-nine miles away.

The streets were lined with people and all the school children had been issued Red Chinese flags. Since we were the first car they all waved them furiously. We responded with the slight bows and dignified gestures that the occasion called for.

We motored beyond Muree, which is at an elevation of six thousand feet, to the general's cabin at nine thousand feet, but were not affected by the high altitude.

The general is a very intelligent, well-traveled man. Since retiring from the Army he had started several private businesses.

There was still snow in patches around his cabin, but we were comfortable before an open fire while we enjoyed the delicious lunch that he provided. Seldom have we had a more interesting conversation.

Our last day in Rawalpindi, Mary was invited to have tea with President Ayub and his daughter. Mary had met Ayub in Washington and later in Pakistan in 1961. His daughter is married to the son of the Wali of Swat and we had been invited to visit her and her husband in Swat, but our plans were changed when she had to come to 'Pindi to help entertain the Chinese.

Mary spent more than an hour with President Ayub, who seemed glad to see her again. He talked freely and confidentially of the war with India and of Pakistan's relations with the Chinese and Americans. He had not known of the handbill being distributed in Lahore during the Chinese visit. It ended:

> Who supported in the hour of need?
> Who betrayed at the time of trial
> Who is friend and who is foe
> It is no longer difficult to know.
> Love the friend and kick the foe
> Welcome China, Yankees go.

President Ayub seemed upset when Mary showed it to him. "Of course," he said, "the government had nothing to do with it." Naturally, Mary believed him.

Forces had been let loose that might be hard to control. Pakistan was boarding the Chinese ship as others were leaving or being dragged off—for example, Sukarno.

How impoverished China could help them as much as rich America was hard to understand. But in the late winter of 1966 Pakistan seemed determined to "cut off its nose to spite its face."

But not before it had thumbed it at Uncle Sam.

Our last night in Rawalpindi was a quiet one as we were leaving early the next morning for Baghdad.

Epilogue

As THE reader must have observed we have been more interested in people than in things. We have naturally enjoyed and appreciated the beauty and diversity of the architecture and ruins of the past, but the people and their different customs fascinated us.

We spent as much time as possible among them—not only in the market places, on the city streets and in village lanes but also in their homes. Whenever feasible we walked. (Only politicians make human contacts from automobiles.) Where there was boat life we spent hours on the docks or being paddled about in sampans.

Everything was strange and different and intriguing. But less so on each visit to Asia or Africa. In the markets betel nuts are being replaced by toothpaste. Lateen sails are giving way to noisy outboard motors. Beautiful saris and Au

Dais are waging a losing battle with Western clothing. The East is not as mysterious as it used to be and only the animals in Africa are not changing.

The people, however, have retained their warm friendliness and charm. The more primitive the country, the nicer the people.

If you are interested in diversity in customs, dress, housing and living, hurry to Asia or Africa before it is too late. The four-hundred-passenger airplane is here.